5

A
Cumbrian
Anthology

compiled by
George Bott

164 Sombrous Gill (w Wordsworth
Rawnsley
226
215 Strangers at the lakes
201 Fragrant Rushes Rev Owen Lloyd
186
146 The Drowned Village
J Richardson

BOOKCASE

129 Ruskin

The Pictures

The pictures are taken from "Views of the Lakes" published by J. Garnet of the Post-Office, Windermere, in 1873. The engravings were by William Banks of Edinburgh. William Banks and his sons drew 26 of the views and the remaining 4 were the work of L. Aspland.

Chapter 1: PROSPECT

Windermere from near Storrs

It is a wild place, and yet there is a pervading spirit of refinement over it all - as if Nature had here wrought her wonders in the mood of the finest art. And at the same time it is a place of infinite variety. The whole territory occupied by the lakes and mountains of this famous district is not more than fifty miles square yet within this limit, comparatively narrow, are comprised all possible beauties of land and water that the most passionate devotee of natural loveliness could desire.

William Winter: *Gray Days and Gold,* 1909

5

Its Beauty Must be Seen

The Lake District has never lacked lyrical tributes.

The character of the scenery is highly romantic, and in no other portion of the United Kingdom can be found - within a similar extent of country - mountains presenting such picturesque outlines and varied forms. To the lover of nature a more attractive tour than this district offers does certainly not exist; whilst the antiquarian, geologist, and botanist will find abundant attractions amongst its mountains and valleys. It is utterly impossible to convey any adequate idea in words of the magnificent scenery which unfolds itself to the view during the tour - no written description could possibly do it justice. To thoroughly comprehend its beauty it must be seen.

John Bradbury: *The English Lakes and how to see them for 5½ Guineas*, 1872.

The Noblest and most Sublime Recreation

Peter Crosthwaite kept a museum in Keswick at the end of the eighteenth century. He never missed an opportunity to publicise both his business and the attractions of the Lake District. On 24 June 1782, he wrote to the Editor of the General Evening Post:

Sir,

Charmed beyond description with the unparalleled scenes I have beheld in Cumberland and Westmorland, please to let your Paper convey my ideas from shore to shore: enchanting lakes, and stupendous mountains; verdant plains, tremendous rocks, waving woods, sweeping cataracts, natural castles, Roman camps, and the little hills, all at once conspire to raise the traveller's admiration and surprize! Here the contemplating Philosopher will meet with his heart's desire! The gay tourer with pleasures he never experienced before! The Valetudinarian may here meet with health! and the Unfortunate with calm repose! In this quarter are found almost endless scenes of matchless beauty, majestic grandeur, and delight. Brown, Pennant, Hutchinson, Gray, Young, West, and many others, have written seemingly in raptures on the various beauties of this uncommon part; and have acknowledged themselves unable to delineate, with either pen or pencil, pictures equal to half its glory! Nor is it wanting in other respects: there is scarce one necessary of life it does not produce; and all excellent in their kind; the viands are exquisite; the air salubrious in general, and fit for almost any constitution; as, in the course of one mile, we can breathe the moist, the middle state, and the pure; the warm, the temperate, and the cold. Hence it comes to pass, that this part is well adapted for the country residence of Noblemen and Gentlemen: and here they have begun to purchase, build, and settle. The many different heights, soils, and waters, afford an ample field for the noble study of botany, and of fossils; the recreations of angling, hunting, fowling, etc. The lakes and rivers, for sailing, shooting, fishing and skating; and lofty Skiddaw (easy of Access) affords one of the grandest variegated prospects in nature! Hither great numbers of the Nobles and Gentry tour, (increasing yearly) and patriot like, spend their Money at home; where their actions demonstrate they are not disappointed in their touring expectations. The Inns are enlarging, good roads mending, singular museums, gardens, etc. furnishing; and many other inventions executing, in order to render this Northern Tour much more entertaining than the Continent. I have in my travels seen two parts of the world, but all fell far short of this magnificent place, and conclude it capable of giving the noblest and most sublime recreation, even to an Eastern Prince, or any other Potentate on earth.

I am, Sir, your very obedient servant,
Peter Crosthwaite,
Admiral of Keswick Lake & Guide &
Companion to Tourers and Lakers.

General Evening Post, 24th June, 1782.

7

Crags and Cataracts

The luscious prose of early writers could conceal genuine admiraton.

You can hardly form a conception of the scenery of many of the striking parts of Cumberland and Westmorland. At the foot of the mountains, steep water-courses run up high among the rocks and clefts mantled with the freshest verdure, with here and there a stunted tree; and then there are larger gulfs and fissures, down which to look from their craggy edges would make the brain giddy. Here a beetling rock and there a wooded shelf of land crowns the heights, while the sunny sky, or the dark clouds of the gathering storm above, give an added interest to the striking scene . . . Oh, it was a fine sight at times, to see the vale below, with its silvery stream and endless cascades, shut in by the many-coloured rocks, that rise up, ridge after ridge, and peak upon peak, all bathed in the hazy light of an autumnal sun, while the dark shadows of the mountains threw a solemn influence around. The water-falls lifted up their voices in the solitude, and the receding hills mingled with the distant sky.

George Mogridge: *Loiterings among the Lakes of Cumberland and Westmorland,* 1849.

Spring is Sprung

When is the best time to visit the Lakes? After the bleakness of winter, perhaps?

Lakeland just now is clad in the rich warm colouring of the coming summer. The heavy rains have given a brilliant freshness to the pasture and buds are bursting on hedge and tree, while the woodland is rapidly covering itself with a mantle of green. The evenings are lengthening, too, and the plaintive call of the cuckoo has been a frequent sound as the nights have closed in. It is perhaps during this transition period, so to speak, from spring to summer, that the wild, indescribable beauty of the Lakes makes itself most deeply felt. When the hills are losing their bleakness, and the water is beginning to reflect a calmer, serener blue, while around may be heard the singing of birds and all the various indescribable sounds by which Nature makes itself known through the gradual, almost imperceptible change that is going on, it is then that the mind of the most callous and hardened materialist is forced to acknowledge that the Lake District possesses a powerful fascination, a power of its own that cannot be found in any other part of our native land.

Westmorland Gazette, 12 May 1899.

The Year Round

Every season has its own charm.

Visiting the Lakes depends much upon the taste of the Tourist. They may be seen with pleasure at any time from the beginning of May to the end of October, provided the weather be favourable. Pedestrians will feel the month of May an agreeable season, and they will then find more room at the inns. Towards the end of June, many professional gentlemen are at liberty, and students at the Universities often find it advantageous to spend three months among the Lakes; thus blending instruction with healthy recreation. Large parties commonly require more time in fitting out and are later in arrival: so that the most busy time is generally from the last week in July to the middle of September. The artist will prefer the richly diversified colouring of autumn, which will be in the greatest perfection in the month of October.

To such as make the tour with a disposition to be pleased, every season has its peculiar charms. The budding spring, the blooming summer, the luxuriant autumn, and even the biting frosts of winter have each their respective attractions. In spring, all nature is in her most cheerful mood: it is pleasing to observe the daily progress of the various kinds of trees as they spread out their leaves, and the different plants as they expand their blossoms; while the feathered choir enliven the air with their morning and

Coniston from the Wood above Bank Ground

evening songs.

In the middle of summer, all is gay; the heat of the sun may at times incommode, but the lengthened days will afford a few hours for retirement in the shade, and the evenings are free from the chilling blasts prevalent at other seasons. In autumn, the fields, the woods, and the mountain sides display the most splendid variety of colouring, and the air is often favourable for distant prospects; but the days are somewhat contracted, and for long excursions more early rising is required. Even in winter, the lakes still exhibit the same expanse of water, or else a glassy sheet of ice; the mountains - whether naked or partially or wholly covered with a mantle of snow - still reign in their wonted majesty; the rocks have lost nothing of their grandeur, and the waterfalls are occasionally rendered more striking by the splendent and fantastic forms in which their spray is congealed.

But it should be kept in mind that more rain falls in mountainous

10

than in open countries and the showers come on more suddenly. The time of the tourist should, therefore, be so calculated as to allow him now and then a spare day; as there is a probability that the greatest part of a day will be sometimes of necessity spent within doors - when the museums and exhibitions of natural and artificial curiosities will be the principal resources.

Jonathon Otley: *Concise Description of the English Lakes*, 1843 .

Winter Magic

Writing from Keswick in February, 1804 to his friend, Miss Barker, Robert Southey focuses on the delights of Lakeland in the winter.

Summer is not the season for this country. Coleridge says, and says well, that then it is like a theatre at noon. There are *no goings on* under a clear sky; but at all other seasons there is such shifting of shades, such islands of light, such columns and buttresses of sunshine, as might almost make a painter burn his brushes, as the sorcerers did their books of magic when they saw the divinity which rested upon the apostles. The very snow, which you would perhaps think must monotonise the mountains, gives new varieties; it brings out their recesses and designates all their inequalities, it impresses a better feeling of their height, and it reflects such tints of saffron, or fawn, or rose-colour to the evening sun. *O Maria Santissima!* Mount Horeb with the glory upon its summit might have been more glorious but not more beautiful than old Skiddaw in his winter pelisse of ermine. I will not quarrel with frost, though the fellow has the impudence to take me by the nose. The lake-side has such ten thousand charms: a fleece of snow or of the hoar frost lies on the fallen trees or large stones; the grass-points, that just peer above the water, are powdered with diamonds; the ice on the margin with chains of crystal, and such veins and wavy lines of beauty as mock all art; and, to crown all, Coleridge and I have found out that stones thrown upon the lake, when frozen, made a noise like singing birds, and when you whirl on it a large flake of ice, away the shivers slide, chirping and warbling like a flight of finches.

John Wood Waiter: *Selections from the Letters of Robert Southey*, 1856.

At Home and Abroad

The scenic attractions of the Lakes vie with those of Europe.

In truth a more pleasing tour than these Lakes hold out to men of leisure and curiosity cannot be devised. We penetrate the Glaciers, traverse the Rhone and the Rhine, while our domestic Lakes of Ullswater, Keswick and Windermere exhibit scenes in so sublime a style, with such beautiful colourings of rock, wood and water, backed with so tremendous a disposition of mountains, that if they do not fairly take the lead of all the views of Europe, yet they are indisputably such as no English traveller should leave behind.

G.A.Cooke: *A Topographical and Statistical Description of the County of Cumberland*, 1803.

Easy Viewing

James Payn offers a little comfort to those visitors who can no longer climb the fells.

We are now going to give a very heterodox piece of advice, but it is one that is founded upon a long experience of Lakeland and other mountain districts. Unless you have plenty of time to spare for seeing natural beauties - plenty of overtime, that is - upon no account waste any of it in ascending a very high mountain. The fatigue, to persons of average strength and ordinary habits, is in much over-proportion to the advantage in any case, while, in nine cases (at least) out of ten, in this part of the country a day sufficiently clear for seeing any great extent of prospect does not occur. There is, of course, some satisfaction in designating more prudent persons as "coddles" and "muffs," but you can do that in a very superior manner (with a little confidence) without having earned the right of insult by any such exertions. A much lower and more easily attained elevation has often a prospect nearly as extensive and infinitely more distinct.

James Payn: *A Hand-Book to the English Lakes*, 1859

Shadow and Substance

Charles and Mary Lamb visited Keswick in 1802 and thought they had 'got into fairyland'. Robert Southey, writing to his friend, Grosvenor Bedford, on 16 February 1804 echoed the Lambs' response.

I have seen a sight more dreamy and wonderful than any scenery that fancy ever yet devised for Faery-land. We had walked down to the lake side; it was a delightful day, the sun shining, and a few white clouds banging motionless in the sky. The opposite shore of Derwentwater consists of one long mountain, which suddenly terminates in an arch thus U, and through that opening you see a long valley between mountains and bounded by mountain beyond mountain; to the right of the arch the heights are more varied and of greater elevation. Now, as there was not a breath of air stirring, the surface of the lake was so perfectly still that it became one great mirror, and all its waters disappeared; the whole line of shore was represented as vividly and steadily as it existed in its actual being - the arch, the vale within, the single houses far within the vale, the smoke from their chimneys, the farthest hills, and the shadow and substance joined at their bases so indivisibly that you could make NO separation even in your judgment. As I stood on the shore, heaven and the clouds seemed lying under me; I was looking down into the sky, and the whole range of mountains, having one line of summits under my feet and another above me, seemed to be suspended between the firmaments. Shut your eyes and dream of a scene so unnatural and so beautiful. What I have

13

said is most strictly and scrupulously true; but it was one of those happy moments that can seldom occur, for the least breath stirring would have shaken the whole vision and at once unrealized it. I have before seen a partial appearance, but never before did, and perhaps never again may, lose sight of the lake entirely; for it literally seemed like an abyss of sky before me, not fog and clouds from a mountain, but the blue heaven spotted with a few fleecy pillows of cloud, that looked placed there for angels to rest upon them.

John Dennis: *Robert Southey - the Story of his Life Written in his Letters*, 1894.

The Heavenly Vision

A century previously, in a very different style, Professor John Wilson (Christopher North), who lived near Windermere, paid his tribute to Lakeland in "My Cottage".

Then ever shall the day that led me here
Be held in blest rememberance. I shall see,
Even at my dying hour, the glorious sun
That made Winander one wide wave of gold,
When first in transport from the mountain-top
I hailed the heavenly vision! Not a cloud.
Whose wreaths lay smiling in the lap of light,
Not one of all those sister-isles that sleep
Together, like a happy family
Of beauty and of love, but will arise
To cheer my parting spirit, and to tell
That Nature gently leads into the grave
All who have read her heart and keep their own
In kindred holiness.

John Wilson: *Lakeland Poems*, 1902.

A National Possession

In the early 1800s, Wordsworth suggested the Lake District was 'a sort of national property, in which every man has a right and interest who has an eye to perceive and a heart to enjoy'. At the end of the century, when Thirlmere was transformed into a reservoir, a similar suggestion was made. It was not until 1951, however, that the Lake District was designated a National Park.

The Lake District is a national possession, unique in England and, in some respects perhaps, in the world. It would be difficult to find elsewhere any portion of the earth's surface where, on a small scale, all the elements of beauty and grandeur, of form and grouping, are so harmoniously combined; where so much variety is comprised within so small a compass, and all is so easily accessible. The smallness of the scale, and the delicate completeness and finish with which Nature has clothed her work, make it peculiarly liable to injury from the rash interference of man, as may be seen in many a spot of perfect natural beauty, which has been marred by incongruous human works - unavoidably, perhaps, in themselves - but carried out with a painful disregard of taste and fitness. A Government having an enlightened regard for the highest interests of the governed might well take such a region under its special protection.

Manchester and Thirlmere Water Scheme: The Case of the Thirlmere Defence Association, n.d.

Sad Little Huts

Celia Fiennes (1662-1741) was one of the earliest visitors to the Lake District. She came in 1698, an intrepid and observant traveller, whose journals are particularly important for their comments on the social and domestic scene.

Here [near Windermere] I came to villages of sad little huts made

15

up of dry walls, only stones piled together and the roofs of same slate; there seemed to be little or no tunnels for their chimneys and have no mortar or plaster within or without; for the most part I took them at first sight for a sort of houses or barns to fodder cattle in, not thinking them to be dwelling houses, they being scattering houses, here one, there another; in some places there may be 20 or 30 together and the churches the same; it must needs be very cold dwellings but it shews something of the laziness of the people; indeed, here and there there was a house plastered, but there is sad entertainment, that sort of clap bread and butter and cheese and a cup of beer all one can have. They are 8 mile from a market town and their miles are tedious to go both for illness of way and length of the mile.

They reckon it but. 8 mile from the place I was at the night before but I was 3 or 4 hours at least going it; here I found a very good smith to shoe the horses, for these stony hills and ways pulls off a shoe presently and wears them as thin that it was a constant charge to shoe my horses every 2 or 3 days; but this smith did shoe them so well and so good shoes that they held some of the shoes 6 weeks. The stoniness of the ways all here about teaches them the art of making good shoes and setting them on fast.

Celia Fiennes *Through England on a Side Saddle in the time of William and Mary*, 1888.

16

Chapter 2: PIONEERS AND THE PICTURESQUE

Leaths Water

Picturesque - a term expressive of that peculiar kind of beauty which is agreeable in a picture

William Gilpin: *Essay upon Prints*, 1768.

Fish and Bread

Windermere char has always been a local delicacy; clap bread was a staple Cumbrian food.

The water [of Windermere] is very clear and full of good fish, but the char fish being out of season could not easily be taken, so I saw none alive; but of other fish I had a very good supper. The season of the char fish is between Michaelmas and Christmas: at that time I have had of them which they pot with sweet spices. They are as big as a small trout, rather slenderer and the skin full of spots, some reddish, and part of the whole skin and the fin and the tail is red like the fins of a perch, and the inside flesh looks as red as any salmon. If they are in season, their taste is very rich and fat, though not so strong or clogging as the lampreys are, but it's as fat and rich a food . . .

Here it was I saw the oat clap bread made. They mix their flour with water so soft as to roll it in their hands into a ball and then they have a board made round and something hollow in the middle, rising by degrees all round to the edge a little higher, but so little as one would take it to be only a board warped. This is to cast out the cake thin and so they clap it round and drive it to the edge in a due proportion till drove as thin as a paper; and still they clap it and drive it round, and then they have a plate of iron same size with their clap board, aud so shove off the cake on it and so set it on coals and bake it. When enough on one side, they slide it off and put the other side. If their iron plate is smooth and they take care their coals or embers are not too hot but just to make it look yellow, it will bake and be as crisp and pleasant to eat as any thing you can imagine. But, as we say of all sorts of bread, there is a vast deal of difference in what is housewifely made and what is ill made: so this, if it's well mixed and rolled up and but a little flour on the outside which will dry on and make it mealy, is a very good sort of food. This is the sort of bread they use in all these countries, and in Scotland they break into their milk or broth or else sup that up and bite of their bread between while. They spread butter on it and eat it with

18

their meat. They have no other sort of bread, unless at market towns and that is scarce to be had unless the market days. So they make their cake and eat it presently, for it's not so good if 2 or 3 days old. It made me reflect on the description made in scripture of their kneading cakes and baking them on the hearth whenever they had company come to their houses, and I cannot but think it was after this manner they made their bread in the old times, especially those eastern countries where their bread might be soon dried and spoiled.

Celia Fiennes: *Through England on a Side Saddle in the time of William and Mary*, 1888.

Unhospitable Terror

In 1724, Daniel Defoe set off on a long exploratory tour of Britain: the narrative of his travels has been described as "by far the most graphic contemporary account of the state of economic and social affairs near the beginning of the eighteenth century". Wlien he reached north Lancashire, he found a landscape very different from that of Robinson Crusoe's.

Nor were these hills high and formidable only, but they had a kind of unhospitable terror in them. Here were no rich, pleasant valleys between them, as among the Alps; no lead mines and veins of rich ore, as in the Peak; no coal pits, as in the hills about Halifax: much less gold as in the Andes, but all barren and wild, of no use or advantage either to man or beast. Indeed, here was formerly, as far back as Queen Elizabeth, some copper mines, and they wrought them to good advantage; but whether the vein of ore failed, or what else was the reason, we know not, but they are all given over long since, and this part of the country yields little or nothing at all . . .

Here we entered Westmoreland, a country eminent only for being the wildest, most barren and frightful of any that I have passed over in

England, or even in Wales itself; the west side, which borders on Cumberland, is indeed bounded by a chain of almost unpassable mountains, which, in the language of the country, are called Fells, and these are called Furness Fells, from the famous promontory beating that name, and an abbey built also in ancient times, and called Furness.

Daniel Defoe: *A Tour through the Whole Island of Great Britain, 1724-6.*

Beauty and Horror

The early visitors to the Lake District, were, broadly speaking, the artists who came in search of the Picturesque and the tourists who came in search of the Romantic. The picturesque way of looking at scenery was to assess its suitability as a picture, using a set of rules clearly defined by the arch apostle of the picturesque, William Gilpin. Here he takes a critical look at Derwentwater.

Of all the lakes in these romantic regions, the lake we are now examining [Derwentwater] seems to be most generally admired. It was once admirably characterized by an ingenious person who, on his first seeing it, cried out, *Here is beauty indeed - Beauty lying in the lap of Horror!* We do not often find a happier illustration. Nothing conveys an idea of *beauty* more strongly than the lake; nor of *horror*, than the mountains; and the former *lying in the lap* of the latter, expresses in a strong manner the mode of their combination. The late Dr Brown, who was a man of taste, and had seen every part of this country, singled out the scenery of this lake for its peculiar beauty. And unquestionably it is, in many places, very sweetly romantic, particularly along its eastern and southern shores; but to give it *pre-eminence* may be paying it too high a compliment, as it would be too rigorous to make any but a few comparative objections.

In the first place, its form, which in appearance is circular, is less interesting, I think, than the winding sweep of Windermere and some other lakes, which, losing themselves in vast reaches behind some cape or promontory, add to their other beauties the varieties of distance and perspective. Some people object to this, as touching rather on the character of the river. But does that injure its beauty? And yet I believe there are very few rivers which form such reaches as the lake of Windermere.

To the formality of its shores may be added the formality of its islands. They are round, regular and similar spots as they appear from most points of view, formal in their situation, as well as in their shape, and of little advantage to the scene. The islands of Windermere are in themselves better shaped, more varied and, uniting together, add a beauty and contrast to the whole.

But the greatest objections to this lake is the abrupt and broken line in several of the mountains which compose its screens (especially on the western and on part of the southern shore), which is more remarkable than on any of the other lakes. We have little of the easy sweep of a mountain-line: at least the eye is hurt with too many tops of mountains, which injure the ideas of simplicity and grandeur. Great care therefore should be taken in selecting views of this lake. If there is a littleness even amidst the grand ideas of the original, what can we expect from representations on paper or canvas? I have seen some views of this lake, injudiciously chosen or taken on too extensive a scale, in which the mountains appear like haycocks.

William Gilpin: *Observations relative chiefly to picturesque beauty made in the year 1772*, 1786.

Heavy Lumps and Murky Spots

William Gilpin gives some advice to devotees of the picturesque on how to judge islands.

The *islands* fall next under our view. These are either a beauty or a deformity to the lake, as they are shaped or stationed.

If the island be round or of any other regular form, or if the wood upon it be thick and heavy (as I have observed some planted with a close grove of Scotch fir) it can never be an object of beauty. At *hand* it is a heavy lump; at a *distance* a murky spot.

Again, if the island (however beautifully shaped or planted) be seated in the centre of a round lake, in the focus of an oval one or in any other *regular* position, the beauty of it is lost, at least in some points of view.

But when its lines and shapes are both irregular, when it is ornamented with ancient oak rich in foliage but light and airy, and when it takes some irregular situation in the lake, then it is an object truly beautiful - beautiful in itself as well as in composition. It must, however, be added that it would be difficult to place such an object in any situation that would be *equally* pleasing from every stand.

William Gilpin *Observations relative chiefly to picturesque beauty made in the year 1772,* 1786.

A Magnet for Poet and Painter

Visitors came, aware of what to expect and conditioned by the extravagant and exaggerated descriptions written by their contemporaries.

> Where Cumbria's mountains in the north arise,
> Where cloud-capped Skiddaw seeks the azure skies,
> Nature hath showered from forth her lavish hand
> Her choicest beauties o'er the favoured land.
> There verdant hills the fertile vales divide,
> And at their base pellucid rivers glide;
> Or the broad lake, outstretched in wide expanse.
> Discovers to the traveller's wondering glance
> Enchanting scenes, which captivate the soul,
> And make therein delightful visions roll.

There the bleak crags their barren bosoms bare,
Stupendous cataracts hideous chasms wear,
From rock to rock they force their headlong way,
Stun with their noise and fill the air with spray;
The hanging cliff its dreadful safety yields,
Where Jove's proud bird its annual eyrie builds.
Thither, attracted from their peaceful home,
The Poet and the Painter love to roam,
Feed fancy full, 'till fraught with fire divine.
Their beauties on the page and canvas shine.
There, too, the botanist, with prying eyes,
Culls the fair flowers in all their thousand dyes;
The teeming waters yield the scaly race,
And the keen spoilsman joins the noisy chase.
Health, rosy goddess, there unharmed resides,
And Liberty, the mountain nymph presides.
Each season there delighted myriads throng
To pass their time these charming scenes among:
For pleasure, knowledge, many thither hie;
For fashion, some, and some - they know not why.
And these same visitors, e'en one and all,
The natives by the name of Lakers call.

James Plumptre *The Lakers: a Comic Opera in three acts*, 1798.

Savage Grandeur

One of the most popular publications for the Lakers was John Dalton's "Descriptive Poem" (1755).

Horrors like these at first alarm,
But soon with savage grandeur charm,
And raise to noblest thoughts the mind:
Thus by thy fall, Lowdore, reclined.

The craggy cliff, impendent wood,
Whose shadows mix o'er half the flood.
The gloomy clouds, which solemn sail,
Scarce lifted by the languid gale,
O'er the capped hill, and darkened vale;
The ravening kite and bird of Jove
Which round the aerial ocean rove,
And, floating on the billowy sky,
With full expanded pinions fly,
Their fluttering or their bleating prey
Thence with death-dooming eye survey;
Channels by rocky torrents torn.
Rocks to the lake in thunders borne,
Or such as o'er our heads appear
Suspended in their mid career,
To start again at his command
Who rules fire, water, air and land,
I view with wonder and delight.
A pleasing, though an awful sight:
For, seen with them, the verdant isles
Soften with more delicious smiles,
More tempting twine their opening bowers,
More lively glow the purple flowers,
More smoothly slopes the border gay,
In fairer circles bend the bay.
At last, to fix our wandering eyes,
Thy roofs, O Keswick, brighter rise,
The lake, and lofty hills between,
Where giant Skiddaw shuts the scene.

John Dalton: *A Descriptive Poem addressed to Two Ladies at their return from viewing the mines near Whitehaven*, 1755.

Beauty, Horror and Immensity Combined

John Brown (1715 - 1766) compares Derwentwater and Keswick with Dovedale in Derbyshire.

Instead of the narrow strip of valley which is seen at Dovedale, you have at Keswick a vast amphitheatre, in circumference about twenty miles. Instead of a meagre rivulet, a noble living lake, ten miles round, of an oblong form, adorned with a variety of wooded islands. The rocks indeed of Dovedale are finely wild, pointed and irregular; but the hills are both little and unanimated; and the margin of the brook is poorly edged with weeds, morass and brushwood. But at Keswick, you will, on on one side of the lake, see a rich and beautiful landscape of cultivated fields, rising to the eye in fine inequalities, with noble groves of oak happily dispersed and climbing the adjacent hills, shade above shade, in the most various and picturesque forms.

On the opposite shore, you will find rocks and cliffs of stupendous height hanging broken over the lake in horrible grandeur, some of them a thousand feet high; the woods climbing up their steep and shaggy sides where mortal foot never yet approached. On these dreadful heights, the eagles build their nests; a variety of water-falls are seen pouring from their summits and tumbling in vast sheets from rock to rock in rude and terrible magnificence, while on all sides of this immense amphitheatre the lofty mountains rise round, piercing the clouds in shapes as spiry and fantastic as the very rocks of Dovedale.

To this I must add the frequent and bold projection of the cliffs into the lake, forming noble bays and promontories; in other parts they finely retire from it and often open in abrupt chasms or cliffs through which at hand you see rich and cultivated vales, and beyond these at various distances mountain rising over mountain, among which new prospects present themselves in mist, till the eye is lost in agreeable perplexity.

Were I to analyse the two places into their constituent principles, I should tell you that the full perfection of Keswick consists of three circumstances, *beauty, horror and immensity* united, the second of which is alone found in Dovedale. Of beauty it hath little, nature having left it almost a desert; neither its small extent nor the diminutive and lifeless forms of the hills admit magnificence.

But to give you a complete idea of these three perfections as they are joined in Keswick would require the united powers of Claude, Salvator and Poussin. The first should throw his delicate sunshine over the cultivated vales, the scattered cots, the groves, the lake and wooded islands. The second should dash out the horror of the rugged cliffs, the steeps, the hanging woods and foaming water-falls; while the grand pencil of Poussin should crown the whole with the majesty of the impending mountains.

John Brown: A Description of the Lake at Keswick, 1767.

Chaos and Old Night

Perhaps the best-known account by a Laker of a journey in one of the valleys is that of Thomas Gray in 1769.

We entered Borrowdale; the crags named Lowdore-banks begin now to impend terribly over the way, and more terribly when you hear that three years since an immense mass of rock, tumbled at once from the brow, barred all access to the dale (for this is the only road) till they could work their way through it. Luckily no one was passing by at the time of the fall, but down the side of the mountain and far into the lake, lie dispersed the huge fragments of this ruin in all shapes and in all directions. Something farther we turned aside into a coppice, ascending a little in front of Lowdore water-fall. The height appeared to be about 200 feet, the quantity of water not great, though (these three days excepted) it hath rained daily for nearly two months before. But then the stream was nobly broken, leaping from rock to rock and foaming with fury . . .

We descended again and passed the stream over a rude bridge.

Borrowdale near the Bowder Stone

Soon after we came under Gowdar-crag, a hill more formidable to the eye and to the apprehension than that of Lowdore, the rocks at top deep-cloven perpendicularly by the rain, hanging loose and nodding forwards, seen just starting from their base in shivers. The whole way down and the road on both sides is strewed with piles of the fragments, strangely thrown across each other and of a dreadful bulk. The place reminds me of those passes in the Alps where the guides tell you to move with speed and say nothing, lest the agitations of the air should loosen the snows above and bring down a mass that would overwhelm a caravan. I took their counsel here and hastened on in silence . . .

The dale opens about four miles higher, till you come to Seathwaite, where lies the way, mounting the hill to the tight, that leads to the wad-mines. All further access is here barred to prying mortals, only there is a little path winding over the fells and for some weeks in the year passable to the dalesmen. But the mountains know well that these innocent people will not reveal the mysteries of their ancient kingdom, *"the reign Chaos and Old Night"*; only I learned that this

27

dreadful road, divided again, leads one branch to Ravenglass and the other to Hawkshead.

Thomas Gray: The Poems, 1775.

Sublime Scenes

Mrs Ann Radcliffe (1764-1823), popular author of gothic novels, went up Skiddaw and wrote an account of her climb: it has many of the characteristics of her fiction.

At length, as we ascended, Derwent-water dwindled on the eye to the smallness of a pond, while the grandeur of its amphitheatre was increased by new ranges of dark mountains, no longer individually great but so from accumulation - a scenery to give ideas of the breaking up of a world. Other precipices soon hid it again but Bassenthwaite continued to spread immediately below us, till we turned into the heart of Skiddaw and were enclosed by its steeps. We had now lost all track, even of the flocks that were scattered ever these tremendous wilds. The guide conducted us by many curvings among the heathy hills and hollows of the mountain, but the ascents were such that the horses panted in the slowest walk and it was necessary to let them rest every six or seven minutes . . .

The mountain soon again shut out all prospect but of its own valleys and precipices covered with various shades of turf and moss and with heath, of which a dull purple was the prevailing hue. Not a tree nor bush appeared on Skiddaw, nor even a stone wall any where broke the simple greatness of its lines. Sometimes we looked into tremendous chasms where the torrent, heard roaring long before it was seen, had worked itself a deep channel and fell from ledge to ledge, foaming and shining amidst the dark rock. These streams are sublime, from the length and precipitancy of their course, which, hurrying the sight with them into the abyss, act as it were in sympathy upon the nerves, and, to save ourselves from following, we recoil from the view with involuntary horror. Of such, however, we saw only two and those by some departure from the usual course up the mountain; but every where met gushing springs till we were within two miles of the summit, when the guide added to the rum in his bottle what he said was the last water we should find in our ascent.

The air now became very thin and the steeps still more difficult of ascent; but it was often delightful to look down into the green hollows of the mountain, among pastoral scenes that wanted only some mixture of wood to render them enchanting.

About a mile from the summit, the way was indeed dreadfully sublime, lying for nearly half a mile along the edge of a precipice that passed with a swift descent for probably near a mile into a glen within the heart of Skiddaw; and not a bush nor a hillock interrupted its vast length or by offering a midway check in the descent, diminished the fear it inspired . . .

How much, too, did simplicity increase the sublimity of this scene in which nothing but mountain, heath and sky appeared! But our situation was too critical or too unusual to permit the just impressions of such sublimity. The hill rose so closely above the precipice as scarcely to allow a ledge wide enough for a single horse. We followed the guide in silence and, till we regained the more open wild, had no leisure for exclamation.

Ann Radcliffe: *A Journey made in the Summer of 1794*, 1795.

New Terror

Goats, apparently, are the most picturesque of animals.

These desolate grounds are very little inhabited. We heard of a design to introduce goats among them, with a view to make Keswick as celebrated for drinking goat's-whey as several of the mountainous parts of Scotland. In some places, indeed, where there are valuable woods, the goat might be a pernicious inmate. But in many places, as we rode, the bare and craggy sides of hills seemed capable of feeding nothing else. Frequent little plots of herbage grow every where among the rocks, inaccesible to any other animal. Even sheep on many of these sloping shelves could find no footing. All this pasturage therefore is lost for want of goats to browse it.

In a picturesque light, no ornament is more adapted to a mountainous and rocky country than these animals. Their colours are beautiful (in those particularly of a darker hue), often playing into each other with great harmony. But among these animals (as among all others) the pied are the most unpleasing, in which opposite colours come full upon each other without any intervening tint.

The shagginess of the goat also is as beautiful as the colours which adorn him, his hair depending in that easy flow which the pencil wishes to imitate.

His actions are still more pleasing. It would add new terror to a scene to see an animal browsing on the steep of a perpendicular rock or hanging on the very edge of a projecting precipice.

William Gilpin: *Observations relative chiefly to picturesque beauty made in the year 1772*, 1786.

The Picturesque Ridiculed

Inevitably, the excesses of the picturesque and the romantic were ridiculed. In "The Lakers," the principal character, Miss Beccabunga Veronica, looks at the landscape with pretentious exaggeration.

The effect is inexpressibly interesting. The amphitheatrical perspective of the long landscape; the peeping points of the many-coloured crags of the head-long mountains, looking out most interestingly from the picturesque luxuriance of the bowery foliage, margining their ruggedness and feathering the fells; the delightful differences of the heterogeneous masses; the horrific mountains, such scenes of ruin and privation! the turfy hillocks, the umbrageous and reposing hue of the copsy lawns, so touchingly beautiful; the limpid lapse of Lowdore, the islands coroneting the flood; the water, the soft purple of the pigeon's neck are so many circumstances of imagery, which all together combine a picture which, for its sentimental beauty and assemblages of sublimity, I never exceeded in the warmest glow of my fancied descriptions. And then the incomparable verdure of turfy slope we are upon; the water bickering at the base; the sultry low of the cattle, sipping the clear wave add a sweet pathos to the magical effect of the surrounding scenery. And now the effulgence of the sunshine landscape is fading away and the blue distances, stealing upon the nearer view, soften the sublime severity. I must take a sketch.

James Plumptre: *The Lakers: a Comic Opera in three acts*, 1798.

Dr Syntax gets a ducking

William Combe's Dr Syntax reached Keswick on his tour in search of the picturesque in 1809.

My Lord now sort the expected chase,
And Syntax in his usual pace,
When four long tedious days had passed,
The town of Keswick reached at last,
Where he his famous work prepared,
Of all his toil the hoped reward.
Soon as the morn began to break,
Old Gristle bore him to the Lake,
Along the banks he gravely paced,
And all its various beauties traced;
When, lo, a threatening storm appeared!
Phoebus the scene no longer cheered;
The dark clouds sunk on every hill;
The floating mists the valleys fill;

Nature, transformed, began to lour,
And threatened a tremendous shower.
"I love," he cried, "to hear the rattle
When elements contend in baltle;
For I insist, though some may flout it,
That we the picturesque may find
In thunder loud, or whistling wind
As often, as I fully ween,
It may be heard as well as seen;
For though a pencil cannot trace
A sound as it can paint a place,
The pen, in its poetic rage,
Can make it figure on the page."
A fisherman who passed that way,
Thought it civility to say -
"An' please you, Sir, 'tis all in vain
To take your prospects in the rain;
On horseback, too, you'll ne'er be able -
'Twere better sure to get a table."
"Thanks," Syntax said, "for your advice,
And faith I'll take it in a trice:
For, as I'm moistened to the skin,
I'll seek a table at the Inn."
But Grizzle, in her haste to pass,
Lured by a tempting tuft of grass,
A luckless step now chanced to take.
And soused the Doctor in the Lake.
But, as it proved, no worse disaster
Befel poor Grizzle and her master,
Than both of them could well endure,
And a warm Inn would shortly cure.
To that warm Inn they quickly hied,
Where Syntax, by the fire-side,

Sat in the Landlord's garments clad,
But neither sorrowful or sad:
Nor did he waste his hours away
But gave his pencil all its play,
And traced the landscapes of the day.

William Combe: The Tour of Dr Syntax in search of the
Picturesque, 1812.

Chapter 3: AT HOME

Wastwater

The pride of descent would blush, were it to be told, that in a recess in the neighborhood of Keswick Lake, a man is now living who enjoys exactly the same property which his lineal ancestor possessed in the reign of Edward the Confessor.

Kearsley's Travelers Guide, 1803

34

Harriet Martineau

Life at Wasdale Head

Ancient customs still lingered in the remote dales a century and a half ago.

The green and perfect level, to which the mountains come down with a sheer sweep, is partly divided off into fields; and a few farmhouses are set down among the fields, on the bends of the gushing and gurgling stream. There is a chapel - the humblest of chapels - with eight pews and three windows in three sides and a skylight over the pulpit. There is also a school. The schoolmaster is entertained on "whittlegate" terms; that is, he boards at the farmhouses in turn. An old man told us that the plan answers. "He gets them on very well," said he; "and particularly in the spelling. He thinks if they can spell, they can do all the rest." Such are the original conclusions arrived at in Wastdale Head it struck us that the children were dirtier than even in other vales, though the houses are so clean that you might eat your dinner off the board or the floor. But the state of the children's skin and hair is owing to the superstition in all these dales; and the schoolmaster is the one who should cure the evil. A young lady who kindly undertook to wash and dress the infant of a sick woman, but who was not experienced in the process, exclaimed at the end, "Oh, dear. I forgot its hands and arms. I must wash them." The mother expressed great horror and said that "if the child's arms were washed before it was six months old, it would be a thief'," and added she, pathetically "I would not like that." The hair and nails must not be cut for a much longer time, for fear of a like result. The Yorkshire people put the alternative of dirty and clean rather strongly in their proverb, "Better hev a bairn wi a mucky feace than wash its noase off;" But the Cumberland folk view the matter more in a moral way, and refuse to have their children baptized into thievery.

Harriet Martineau: *Complete Guide to the English Lakes*, 1855.

Beyond the Threshold

Harriet Martineau takes a peep into a Cumbrian farmhouse in 1850.

There is something in the autumn, as in early spring days, which exhausts one's strength. One looks around for a resting-place after a very few miles. I must ask for a seat in this old farm-house: the seat and the draught of milk are graciously given. My thoughts being turned on the health of the district, it is natural to observe how entirely all conditions of health were overlooked, while those modes of living grew up which are still followed by the country people.

The door here is not high enough for man or woman to enter without stooping; the window is on the same side and there is a dead wall opposite. If there is too little access to the outer air elsewhere, there is too much in the direction of the chimney.

The chimney is a large recess, six feet high and capable of containing three or four persons sitting on each side of the fireplace of the fire which burns on the hearth. A large provision of meat hangs in the smoke and well smoked the meat is likely to be, judging by the soot which hangs upon everything within the recess.

The wicker plastered sides are almost as sooty as the beam and chain from which the boiler is suspended. It is said that the country custom of men sitting bonneted within doors arose from the need of keeping their heads covered from the soot and drought, and even the dirt of the chimney. The fire is of peat; and when the autumn and winter storms pour rain and blast into the wide funnel of the chimney, the soot is brought down in oily streams, which it almost turns one's stomach to see trickling on the wails.

The chambers are no nicer. The "bower", the room of the master and mistress, is extremely small, over the pantry and a little larger. The loft where everybody else sleeps - children, servants and all - has no ceiling, no furniture but the great chests where the oatmeal, the malt, some dried meat and the family cloth are kept; no sheets on the beds, but rugs and blankets for warmth and probably no partition, but a rope carried across the loft, on which are hung the clothes in wear. If there is a partition, it is probably of upright boards through which everything must be heard and everything may be seen.

The young men may wash their faces and hands at the pump every day, for what I know: but from what one sees when their collars are open in warm weather, it seems that they dress as their neighbours, the pitmen at the collieries do on Sundays - put on a clean shirt over a skin which has not felt the touch of water for half a year and more.

The elderly woman now on the settle nursing the infant (her grandchild) is ill and she tells me with a sort of contempt of the advice the clergyman gave her while waiting till the doctor came round. The advice was to put her feet in warm water and go to bed. I asked her if this was not good advice. She says that, in the first place, putting her feet in warm water would send the blood to her head; and, in the next place, that it is thirty years since she washed her feet and it shall be another thirty before she does it again. Seeing me of another way of thinking, she tells me she had a dear daughter who washed her feet once and she died under the age of twenty-five.

Harriet Martineau: *A Fear at Ambleside*, 1850.

House Proud

Cumbrian farmers opted for solid furniture, durable clothes and a simple diet.

The farmhouses are generally very ancient and their interior economy has been but little changed by time. They are generally built of stone with very thick walls and are either thatched or covered with coarse blue slate. The floor of slate is kept scrupulously clean and is ornamented by scroll-work done with red or yellow ochre or chalk according to the taste of the inmates. The great oaken beams are generally polished and bright brass and mahogany often decorate the kitchen. The people in Westmorland and Cumberland are in fact "house proud". The furniture generally consists of a long oaken table with a bench on either side, where the whole family, master, children and servants take their meals together. On one side of the fireplace is generally a seat about six feet long, called the long settle, its back often curiously carved, and a chest with two or three divisions. At the other side of the fireplace is the sconce, a sort of fixed bench, under which one night's elden or fuel is deposited every evening.

The chairs are generally of oak with high arms and carved on the backs. The bedsteads are also of oak with carved testers. The clothing of the family was formerly made from wool spun from the native fleece and of linen made from the flax which was grown on almost every farm; the "hemp ridge" in fields still bears its name, although its origin may have been forgotten. Clogs, or wooden-soled shoes well adapted to a mountainous and rainy country, continue in common use.

These counties being unfavourable to the production of wheat, oats and barley are the principal cereals. The barley grown on the small estates was formerly made into malt and each family brewed its own ale. Wheaten bread, now common, was only used on particular occasions. Small loaves were once given to persons invited to funerals, which they were expected to take home and eat in remembrance of their departed neighbour. Until late years, the use of wheaten bread was almost unknown in a great part of the district, particularly among the mountains. Cakes made of barley and called flat bread, and similar to the *flad bred* of Norway, are still in general use. They are also known by the name *scons*, a word which may be derived from the Old Norse *skan*, a crust. The mountain cheese called *whillimen*, which is so tough that the Cumberland rustics have been facetiously said to shoe their clogs with its rind instead of iron, is an example of the simple and severe diet in which the mountaineers resemble the peasants of Norway; and in that country, as in Cumberland and Westmorland, oatmeal porridge is an article of common consumption.

John Murray: *Handbook for Westmorland, Cumberland and the Lakes*, 1869.

E Lynn Linton

Simple Hospitality

Even in the remotest parts of the district, travellers were welcomed and given food and drink, as here near Haweswater.

At the edge of the moor are the few lonely dwellings, customary with waste places literally taken from the moor-fowl and made to grow potatoes and oats for men and bairns; dwellings and people as little part of the social life of the country as the backwoodsman in his hut is part of the body politic of New York. The people living on the skirts of these wide moors are as peculiar in their way as the dalesfolk; often educated to a scholarly exercise of intellect, while living in a loneliness that is almost eremitical and in a simplicity and poverty that take you back many generations and still more cycles of national civilization.

At one such lonely place - a house standing in the midst of desolation - a homestead literally snatched from the wild - we went in to ask for bread and milk . . . The house was a poor-looking but well-built stone cottage, surrounded by a wall that of itself at once inspired the feeling of loneliness; for it enclosed no gardened space of fruit and flowers, only a neglected barren strip of ground that in the winter would be ankle-deep in mud and in summer was a dusty cart-track thickly grown with weeds and disfigured by all manner of accumulated unsightliness: an utterly unlovely and ungraceful enclosure, meaning defence of a kind only, no more. Indeed, the general aspect of the place was not so much one of poverty or stint as of bleakness and unloveliness; life with the element of artificial or made beauty entirely absent. Of natural beauty even, there was none of the softer or more ornamental kind; only such as could be got out of a wide tract of moorland, with the distant line of hills beyond and the ever-changing aspects of the sky.

There was no bustle of a farmhouse about; no kine lowing, no horses tramping, no bleating of sheep or barking of dogs, and at first not a human being anywhere. But presently, in a little way off, we saw a family group haymaking; and when they saw us standing by the

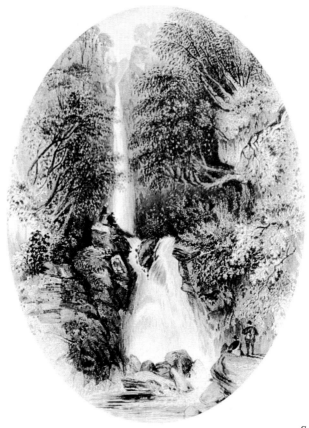

Scaleforce

house-door they left off work and came to know what we wanted.

They were noticeable people, these two "house parents". The man - a mere working farmer tilling his small piece of ground for family consumption mainly, coming in to greet us, hot and weary with his work - was refined and thoughtful; a man evidently well considered in his degree; as his wife said with no little pride, though with feigned displeasure, "chosen to be a juryman oftener than was fair, because they knew him and what a fine scholar he was". She was a ruder person, bright-eyed and bonny but of a less gracious nature; not at the first so frankly hospitable as he - he offering his best with a manly courtesy and an open-handed generosity essentially noble - but she, woman-like, hanging back doubtingly, troubled at the prospect of short-coming in the daytime and reckoning up mouths and loaves with true feminine carefulness.

After a short time, however, she was as kind and generous as her husband but her kindness was from personal magnetism and the quick sympathies of her woman's heart; his from the dignity of his own nature and the service he felt bound by his manhood to render to all men alike. They gave us freely of their best - wheaten bread, butter and a huge jug of milk - and the man took down a large cheese from the "rannel balk" (the beam running across the kitchen) piled up with cheeses for their own use only and told us "to spare nothing, we were kindly welcome". The place was well furnished in its way - the old settle by the chimney neck, the press and clock of black oak, the high-backed chairs giving it a true old-fashioned air and manner of comfort, as understood by these remote farmers. And they were proud of their place, boasting that the Dun Bull (the little inn at Mardale Green) hadn't a room the like of theirs and that they could accommodate more folks than them if they had a mind.

E. Lynn Linton: *The Lake Country*, 1864.

Wretched but Welcoming

On the other side of the district, visitors found a similar welcome in Borrowdale.

Having once more reached the level ground, we turned off, on the left towards Seat Oller (pronounced Si Torr), a solitary and wretched-looking farm-house. Although the exterior of this lonely dwelling does not promise much comfort, its interior is singularly neat, being occupied by a hospitable couple, who cheerfully share their provisions

41

with the wearied tourist, with an affability and politeness that are little expected by travelers from the south of England. For this they make no charge, although they will thankfully accept a gratuity.

J. Farrington & T.H. Horne:*The Lakes of Lancashire, Westmorland and Cumberland*, 1816.

Wordsworth and Whitewash

Wordsworth was not in favour of white cottages; A. C. Gibson, writing just before Wordsworth died, disagreed.

I do maintain that no objects can give such a gratifying air of life and cheerfulness to a valley surrounded or not by high mountains, or so strikingly enhance the bright green of herbage and foliage, or the more sombre but warmer tints of near or distant hills, as a liberal sprinkling over the landscape of pure white cottages, embosomed, as these are, each in its own nest of sheltering trees; and I do wish that the farmers of Langdale and all our other fell-dales would expend a shilling or two annually on lime and bestow upon their romantically situated homesteads "the cleanly, pleasant appearance derivable from a plentiful, periodical application of white-wash".

Their present grim, dingy, almost squalid exteriors are strongly suggestive to the mind of a stranger of internal poverty, desolation and dirt, than which nothing can be more distant from their real in-door condition. For in all these scattered houses, miserable as they look externally, there is abundance for the wants of the inmates and for the requirements of hospitality; and their cleanliness is such that, as I have partaken of many meals spread upon their unclothed tables, so, in the absence of a table, would I not scruple to eat my dinner if laid upon any of their blue flagged floors, for those are cleaner than many table-cloths I have seen in the course of my peregrinations through other countries.

A.C. Gibson: *The Old Man; or Ravings and Ramblings round Coniston*, 1849.

De Quincey and Dove Cottage

Thomas de Quincey moved into Dove Cottage at Grasmere when the Wordsworths left in 1807.

The native Dalesman, well aware of the fury with which the wind often gathers and eddies about any eminence, however trifling its elevation, never thinks of planting his house *there*: whereas the stranger, singly solicitous about the prospect or the range of lake which his gilt saloons are to command, chooses his site too often upon points better fitted for a temple of Eolus (the God of winds) than a human dwelling-place; and he belts his house with balconies and verandas that a mountain gale often tears away in mockery.

The Dalesman, wherever his choice is not circumscribed, selects a sheltered spot which protects him from the wind altogether upon one or two quarters and on all quarters from its tornado violence. He takes good care at the same time to be within a few feet of a mountain beck, a caution so little heeded by some of the villa founders that absolutely, in a country surcharged with water, they have sometimes found themselves driven by sheer necessity to the after-thought of sinking a well.

The very best situation, however, in other respects, may be bad in one, and sometimes find its very advantages and the beetling crags which protect its rear, obstructions the most permanent to the ascent of smoke; and it is in the contest with these natural baffling repellents of the smoke and in the variety of artifices for modifying its vertical or for accomplishing its lateral escape that have arisen the large and graceful variety of chimney models.

My cottage, wanting this primary feature of elegance in the constituents of Westmoreland cottage architecture and wanting also another very interesting feature of the elder architecture, annually becoming more and more rare - viz. the outside gallery (which is sometimes merely of wood but is much more striking when provided for in the original construction of the house and completely *enfoncé* in the masonry) - could not rank high amongst the picturesque houses of the country; those at least which are such by virtue of their architectural form.

It was, however, very irregular in its outline to the rear by the aid of one little projecting room and also of a stable and little barn in immediate contact with the dwelling-house. It had, besides, the great advantage of a varying height, two sides being about fifteen or sixteen feet high from the exposure of both storeys; whereas the other two, being swathed about by a little orchard that rose rapidly and unequally towards the vast mountain range in the rear, exposed only the upper storey, and consequently on those sides the elevation rarely rose beyond seven or eight feet.

All these accidents of irregular form and outline gave to the house some little pretensions to a picturesque character, while its "separable accidents" (as the logicians say), its bowery roses and jessamine clothed it in loveliness - its associations with Wordsworth crowned it to my mind with historical dignity - and, finally, my own twenty-seven years' off-and-on connections with it have by ties personal and indestructible endeared it to my heart so unspeakably beyond all other houses that even now I rarely dream through four nights running that I do not find myself (and others besides) in some one of those rooms and, most probably, the last cloudy delirium of approaching death will re-install me in some chamber of that same humble cottage.

Thomas de Quincey: *Tait's Edinburgh Magazine*, January 1840.

Visible Darkness

In earlier times, rushlights provided illumination (of a kind).

Indeed, this was the only light they used, when they used one at all. The rushes were cut and gathered on the fell and hung up in bundles upon crooks in the kitchen ceiling. For use they were peeled almost but not quite all round, and then dipped in the fat of sheep or rough grease of the house that was saved up for that purpose. When the rush was ready, it was placed in a candlestick which somewhat resembled nippers, and as it burnt on was pushed through. The light shed was at the best but feeble and so did little more than make the darkness visible. And yet people in well-to-do circumstances used the light almost exclusively . . . the grandfather and grandmother of Mr William Cleasby, who lived at Aisgill, did not burn more than one pound of "white candles" in the year.

. . . I have been told the following anecdote of a man who had come from some other parish and saw for the first time a pair of snuffers. He picked them up, looked at them, saw in part their design, and then, snuffing the candle with his finger and thumb, deposited the burnt wick in the box of the snuffers. Then, looking up with the air of a discoverer, remarked, "Very ingenious things".

W. Nicholls: *The History and Traditions of Mallerstang Forest and Pendragon Castle*, 1883.

Not a Pretty Picture

Few tourists, reasonably comfortable in their hotels, can have realised what conditions were like in the towns they were visiting - Keswick, in 1852, for example.

The modern town of Keswick has one *principal* street, it is true; but there are several minor streets and the cottages are built in narrow lanes, in enclosed courts and yards, and in confined passages. Houses and tenements are crowded with foul middens and are encroached upon by privies, with large open cesspools, by pig-sties, stables, cowsheds, and by slaughter-houses. The refuse from all of these places must, in by far the most cases, stagnate or sluggishly pass along the surface channels into the nearest drain, there to taint the subsoil and contaminate alike the earth and air of the neighbourhood.

Most of the houses are built with rubble-stone of the district; some are rough-cast and lime-whited externally. Many of the cottages are small having low ceilings and defective means for ventilation; the ground-floor and basement walls of many houses are damp, in consequence of the subsoil being undrained, and some of the cottage wails are wet to rottenness, and the air of the room is permanently tainted by an abutting cesspool or midden, to the serious injury of the health of the inhabitants. A town may, architecturally, show much external beauty and be in a most defective sanitary state: there is, however, little or none of even architectural beauty in Keswick . . .

Whilst a portion of the inhabitants have water close to their houses, obtainable either by well or pump, others - and these the poor - have no water-right and are obliged to beg water or take it wherever they can get it. At Brigham-row there are 60 persons without any water but that flowing down the river, and 47 of these people have no privy. At the Forge there are 70 persons who have only one open trough to fetch water from and there is only one privy for all these people, besides the work-people. There are two springs of water near the town (one on the Ambleside-road, the other on the Penrith-road): the water from these springs is much used by the inhabitants for brewing and for making tea. The women state that half the weight of tea, if made with this water, will be stronger and better than double the quantity of tea made with the pump-water nearer their houses . . .

The village of Braithwaite, for example, contains, in proportion to its population, more dirt disease and death than any decent town. It is one of the most romantic and filthy villages in England and yet it might easily be made one of the cleanest and neatest . . .

There are five common lodging-houses in Keswick . . . In five years, 22,546 males and 10,568 females, or a total of 33,114 human beings have been lodged one night in the five common-lodging houses of Keswick. These five houses have 12 rooms and 26 beds, or an average of more than two beds to each room. There is no division betwixt the beds in any of the rooms, other than a slight curtain; the beds are within one foot of each other and yet it will be perceived that

22,546 males have associated in rooms and beds so arranged with 10,568 females. This fact alone should induce local attention, as these dangerous outcasts of society live more abundantly in vice and crime than the hard-working labourer can do by honesty. Those who give money readily to prowling beggars would shrink from the lust they abet, the vice they foster and the crime they educate, could the whole amount be shown to them.

Common lodging-houses are kept by a class of persons who pander to the vices of human nature for purposes of pecuniary gain. They charge from 1d. to 3d. per night for each adult person entering their house and this demand complied with, they harbour the known thief, the professional vagrant or the unfortunate outcast. The housebreaker and pickpocket receive shelter countenance and advice; the unlicensed pedlar, the vagrant and the thief are frequently combined in the same person, so that the support supplied by the *so-called* charity is turned to uses of immorality, fraud and crime, reaching occasionally to murder.

Robert Rawlinson: *Report to the General Board of Health on preliminary enquiry into the sewerage, drainage and supply of water, and the sanitary condition of the inhabitants of the town, and township of Keswick,* 1852.

Hard Labour - Small Profits

The life-style of the Cumbrian shepherd is one of extremes, all-too-easily romanticised by the uninitiated.

The whole life of the mountain or Cumbrian shepherd of modern days consists of extremes of laborious and hurried exertions in times of emergency and of comparative ease when the flocks are known to be safe; of the keenest exposures to drifting and blinding snow and hail and to the reflected heat of the narrow valleys; of clambering on hand and knee among the slippery and rugged rocks and of plunging in the mosses or the drifted snows; of boisterous conviviality on a few stated occasions in the year and of long and solitary wanderings among the mists and rain and perils of the dark mountain tops; of the wild and uncontrollable excitement of the loud-echoing tally-ho of a mountain fox chase; and of the still and lonesome watchings, night after night, near the cubs concealed in the fastness of the borran and bield. Now toiling alone up the steep mountain side with a large sack of sheep-hay on his head, against a strong and gusty wind; and now singing "tarry woo" in a full chorus of his brethren, stretched on the sunny greensward after the toils of the washing-day are over; and finally may be added, after the greatest exertions and most anxious care, obtaining the smallest profits of any class of men of equal capital in the kingdom.

But the very extremes of a shepherd's life possess charms which induce a keen rivalry for occupation; and consequently leave a very small if any margin for the savings' bank after the annual payments are made.

William Dickinson: *Essay on the Agriculture of West Cumberland*, 1850.

Chapter 4: SHEPHERDS AND SHEEP

Brothers' Water from near Kirkstone Pass

The Lake sheep are specially curly; they graze on silken lawns and remind one of the souls of the blessed in heaven. Nobody watches them as they spend their time in feeding, sleeping and divine pondering.

Karel Capek: *Letters from England,,* 1925

49

Servants for Hire

Both male and female farm-servants were recruited by farmers at the Hiring Fairs, held twice a year. The female candidates appear to have presented problems.

A custom prevails throughout the county of hiring both male and female farm-servants by the half-year, ending at Whitsuntide and Martinmas. These are fed and lodged in the house, eating at the family table on the smaller farms and working along with the sons and daughters of the farmers. On the larger farms, day or week labourers are employed besides the half-yearly servants and, mostly, separate tables are kept.

Proverbial as farmers have long been rather wrongfully held for complaining, there is no subject on which they can more justly complain than on the wasteful carelessness and incapacity of their female servants. With some few creditable exceptions and others approaching in various degrees to servant-like qualifications, the very large majority of them, though not always indolent, are thoughtless to excess of both their employer's interest and their own credit, their chief object appearing to be to obtain a half-year's home and the means of purchasing gaudy and unserviceable dresses. Trained as they mostly are in the cottages of colliers and other labourers in towns and villages, too often without any kind of education tending to fit them for the servitude they are necessitated to undertake and probably without a single caution from their ignorant parents as to their future moral conduct or a word of instruction as to the duties of servants, they are decked out and sent to the hiring markets to make the best bargain they can. They enter on their servitude lamentably ignorant of most of what they ought to know and it is no wonder that they give rise to almost universal complainants of the untidy and inadequate performance of their duties. It is very evident that this grievance must continue to be felt in its full force until some system can be adopted of providing useful instruction for the classes from which servants spring, beyond the courses now styled education, which barely consists of reading and writing, without a word on the duties which are to constitute the chief employment of their lives.

A very reprehensible practice prevails among the younger men-servants of hiring to several masters on the same day and receiving the customary shilling from each without the intention of entering the service of any of them but intending to hire at some distant market, and leave all but one master to find substitutes as they best can. Masters will surely find it time to put a stop to this obtaining of money under false pretences by resolutely requiring the signature of all strange servants to short printed forms of contract and then magistrates would be in an easy position to enforce the performance.

William Dickinson: *Essay on the Agriculture of West Cumberland*, 1850.

Freedom and Familiarity

This picture of a hiring day at Kendal about the middle of the nineteenth century is probably typical.

The street was well supplied with young men whose want of situation was indicated by a bit of straw, paper or leaf exhibited under their hat-band. The show of female servants at the Cross was unusually small and the demand much greater than the supply. The girls were all ages from thirteen to thirty, looking remarkably healthy and fully maintaining the compliment of the bonny lasses of Westmorland. Most of them were well dressed and exceedingly cheerful.

More good temper could not be wished than was exhibited betwixt buyers and sellers. The bargaining seemed to be on the same principle you see in a cattle market. A number of questions are asked as to age, family, last service, what they can do and wages. "What do you want?" said a farmer to a girl that seemed left at last. "Three guineas but say three pounds; I'll not take less." "Ye're four or five and twenty, ain't you?" "Me!" was her tart reply, "I am just turned sixteen." One man boasting to his neighbour how well he had succeeded, observed, "Aye, she is a fine lass, I ken the breed of her." The girls showed great freedom in asking questions. "Where is your house?" "How many kye (cows) do you keep?" "What is there to do?" One man thought he would secure his end and in answer to the last question said, "Oh, we have nothing to do." "Then I'll not hire with you," was the reply. In a few instances, the mothers were there setting off the claims of a daughter. They would say, "She is a lale (little) un but she is a good un." "Can you milk the kye?" cried a strapping farmer to a young woman. "My wife is on her last legs and I will take you for good." "I can milk nin, an' ye're auld enough to be my grandfather; I'm not gaun to hire for life just now," replied the buxom wench.

Any one familiar with the customs of our hiring fairs and the chaff and banter that goes on between those to hire and those hiring will recognize this as an accurate description, and we are bound to admit that this freedom and familiarity between those who are afterwards to hold the relation of master and servant are not good for either party.

Carlisle Diocesan Conference, August 1873, report - in
Carleolensia, 1873.

A Living Wage

In the middle of the nineteenth century, farm wages were competitive.

In Furness, the agricultural labourers receive comparatively high wages owing to the demand for workmen in the mines. They generally bind themselves half yearly at the fairs or hirings held at Ulverston, Dalton and Broughton every Whitsuntide and Martinmas. Good men now receive on an average from £13 to £14 by the half year and live at the commodious farmhouses, generally sharing the meals (except in some cases breakfast and supper, but always dinner) of their employers and almost living as members of the family. Young men and boys average from about £8 to £10 by the half year and women suitable for farmhouse work and with some knowledge of dairy management average from £5 to £6 by the half year. This is a great increase on the wages paid in the district twenty years ago, which did not exceed £8 half yearly for good men; £5 half yearly for young men and boys; and £4 half yearly for women. The hours of labour in summer are from five in the morning until seven in the evening.

If this custom were better observed throughout the country the fine old feeling between employer and employed, which made them regard each other as having something in common, would not give way to a selfishness which will only bring misery upon both in the end.

G.M. Tweddell: Furness Past and Present, 1870.

Home Ground

Herdwicks are wedded to their heaf - the piece of land where they were born and bred.

A peculiarity of the Herdwicks is their fondness for the heaf upon which they have been bred and accustomed to pasture; so great is their love or homing instinct that special covenants are inserted in all leases relating to the letting of Herdwicks. No obstacle is too great to prevent a Herdwick, which has been sold and removed a dozen or more miles away, returning to its native heaf - they are sad home-wanderers, as many farmers know who have bought them for crossing or winter feeding.

Many an old wether is retained on account of his usefulness in "keeping the heaf" even when his teeth are gone: not only does he keep strangers off but he educates the young sheep of the flocks till they are accustomed to their heaf.

F.W. Garnett: Westmorland Agriculture 1800-1900, 1912.

Spotting a Herdwick

Willliam Dickinson writing in 1852, looks back at Herdwicks.

One hundred years ago, the sheep were nearly all of the grey-faced or black-faced moor or mountain breed. At this period, when nearly half the low-lying district and the whole of the hills and mountains were open common, almost every farm had a frontage to some common or other or access to one by an "outgang" or a narrow strip of open land leading from the village to the common. The Herdwick breed possesses more of the characters of an original race than any other in the county. It stands lowest in the scale of excellence and shows no marks of kindred with any other race. The majority are without horns and their legs and faces are grey or mottled. Where great care is exercised in selecting and breeding, the nose is of a lighter grey and is then termed "raggy" or "rimy" from its resemblance to hoar-frost. Formerly many of this breed had large manes and beards of very coarse grey hair; then fleeces were much mixed with *greys* and *kemps*. These defects are now removed, without any injury to the storm-resisting qualities of the fleece. After heavy rains and strong winds in winter and spring, the wool of the fleeces is turned to almost black, as if drenched with soot and water.

This discolouring of the wool is an indication of the sheep having sustained a sudden and severe check in their thriving. As the weather improves and the sheep begin to thrive, the blackness goes off and the fleece resumes its natural colour. The weight of the fleece varies from 2½ to 3½ lbs.

F.W. Garnett: *Westmorland Agriculture 1800-1900*, 1912.

Clean and Crop

Of all the tasks involved in rearing sheep, shearing or clipping is one of the most vital.

Two things ought to be seen in the lake country: sheep-washing and sheep-shearing - the last by no means so pretty as the first, neither so animated nor so picturesque, but still to be seen by all who have the opportunity. The day before it begins, the sheep and lambs are bleating with more than usual passion, for the dogs are bringing them in off the fells, separating them into lots, and dividing the little ones from their mothers, to the really pathetic distress of both. Then the lambs are left to the care of heaven and the sheep are pent up in a shed together. whence they are dragged out by boys as they are wanted, and flung on their backs into the lap of a clipper seated on a long kind of settle - "sheep forms" they are called - who tranquilly tucks the little pointed head under his arm and clips away at the under part of the wool, taking care to keep the fleece unbroken, the art being to hold the middle way and neither to graze the skin by going too close nor to loosen the fleece by cutting above the welted fibres.

All four feet are now tied together and the beast is hauled round as a solid kind of rug, when its back is sheared in the same way, the fleece hanging down like a bit of carpet or small crib blanket.

When the whole is off, its legs are untied and it is lugged - that is the only word to express it - panting and terrified to the place where the man stands with the ruddle-pot and branding-iron, where it receives its distinctive smear and letter of assignment and is then dismissed to its huddled group of companions clustering together at the remotest spot in the yard available.

This is merely a bald catalogue of the scene; the real portraiture would be very different. For in this must be included the farm buildings overshadowed with trees and the low-roofed farmhouse covered with ivy and bordered with English cottage flowers; the sheep-dogs lying in the sun, with a lazy manner of indifference as having nothing to do, it being holiday time for them and a transfer of responsibility - some about the feet of the men and some stretched wide awake, in fact, however fast asleep in seeming. as outposts by the gates and along the walls, to keep the sheep in closed ranks; the one special strong man - generally a dare-devil looking fellow who might be a smuggler or a poacher but who is only an extra powerful shepherd - whose particular duty seems to be to supply the jokes and rough horseplay and to carry the shorn sheep to the ruddle-pot, for they are difficult to manage now when they have no wool and must be held by sheer strength; the one or two handsome Scandinavian faces, straight and fair, sure to be among the number; the lithe figures of the boys learning of the men and handled gently, even by the roughest; the pretty young house girls, looking so quiet and gentle, dressed in their Sunday best and carrying great jugs of beer - the strongest that can be brewed - laughing and yet shy, as they penetrate into the mass of men and animals in the yard; the cows milking by the byre doors; the purple hills and the calm lake; the home fells whitened with the shorn sheep let loose scattered over them like daisies, but very unhappy yet, not recognised by their lambs and utterly humiliated and ashamed; the harmonious combinations into which all things group themselves, animate and inanimate; and the hot summer sun shining over all: these are the incidents which make sheep-shearing a striking thing to see. But perhaps, for reasons not needed to be particularised, more pleasing if you stand to leeward and out of earshot of what is said.

For the first fortnight in July, you may take your choice of the farms all over the country, large or small, according to your liking, wanting no other guidance than the incessant barking of the sheep dogs and the rough voices of the men directing.

E. Lynn Linton: *The Lake Country*, 1864.

Buried Alive

The shepherd's work would be impossible without the help of his dog.

Some dogs have the faculty of discovering sheep when buried . . . a single dog has been known to point out unerringly the locality of many scores of drifted sheep in a day, even when several of them were at a depth beyond the reach of the shepherd's snow-pole. In the great Martinmas snow-storm of 1807 (by far the heaviest fall within the present century) the writer was personally engaged, though very young, assisting to search for and release about 400 sheep . . .

After a fearful night of tempest and of useless foreboding on the part of the family, at daybreak next morning not a sheep of the flock turned out was to be seen, for every one was drifted over and none could tell where a single sheep was to be found . . .

An untutored sheep-dog, not quite a year old, was one of the party, with three or four older dogs of the same kind. The older dogs took little notice of what was going on but the young one began to be very curious about the proceedings and amid his gambols in the snow, would every now and then return to the working party to peep into and snuff about the holes they made with the poles.

In a little time he seemed to take still greater interest in the work and went from hole to hole, examining and smelling at them as the poles were drawn out . . . He remained looking intently into one of the holes after the men had gone to some distance; and all at once a new light seemed to break in upon him and he began to scratch in the snow with all his might. This was just what was desired and when he was seen to be in earnest, the men returned and dug down through the drift for 7 or 8 feet, encouraging the anxious whelp, and, deeper than their poles would reach, they found a cluster of five or six sheep huddled close together. When these were released, the dog barked and howled with delight . . .

The last living sheep discovered was on New Year's Day. It had taken shelter in a hollow under a whin and had remained in the small space of a 5 feet cave from the 18th of November, with nothing to eat but what it could nibble from the prickly bush; and when liberated on a blight frosty day, it appeared nearly or quite blind.

William Dickinson: *On the Farming of Cumberland Journal of the Royal Agricultural Society of England Vol. XIII*, 1853.

Chapter 5: UNDERGROUND, OVERGROUND

Honister Crag from the Quarry Road to Yew Crag

In kindness to each other, in the proper discharge of the duties of domestic life, in demonstrative respect for those above them, in real civility to strangers, though accompanied perhaps in some instances by gruffness of manner, the mining population of Coniston are not to be surpassed by any other of equal numbers in the world.

A.C. Gibson: *The Old Man,* 1849

A Desolate Waste

The quarries of Honister Pass impressed a traveller in 1749 by their situation.

The whole mountain is called *Unnisterre*, or, as I suppose, *Finisterre* for such it appears to be; myself and only one more of our company determined to climb this second precipice, and in about another hour we gained the summit. The scene was terrifying; not an herb was to be seen, but wild savine growing in the interstices of the naked rocks. The horrid projection of vast promontories; the vicinity of the clouds; the thunder of the explosions in the slate quarries; the dreadful solitude; the distance of the plain below and the mountains heaped on mountains that were piled around us, desolate and waste, like the ruins of a world which we only had survived, excited such ideas of horror as are not to be expressed, We turned from this fearful prospect afraid even of ourselves and bidding an everlasting farewell to so perilous an elevation, we descended to our companions.

Gentleman's Magazine Vol. XXI, February 1751.

A Perilous Trade

A century later, comments were more realistic.

The quarries of Honister Crag produce some of the finest roofing-slate in the kingdom, but the steepness of the precipice makes the labour of working it very perilous, the quarrymen being let down by ropes from the top to enable them to effect a lodgement and commence excavations. The slate was formerly brought down on hurdles on the backs of men, but roads have since been cut on the face of the precipice, admitting of the passage of small sledges. The workmen reside in the quarries, leaving them only on Sundays, and slate-hovels perched upon the ledges of this stupendous cliff give a strange conception of a life passed in so desolate a spot. The slate-quarrier niches himself like a sapper effecting a lodgement in a bastion. He hangs halfway up the mountain, prosecuting his "perilous trade" and is scarcely perceptive to the eye below; but the unceasing click of his hammer is distinctly heard.

John Murray: *Handbook for Westmorland, Cumberland and the Lakes*, 1869.

A Dangerous Descent

A graphic description of 1864 leaves no doubt of the dangers of quarrying on Honister Crag.

The slate quarrying is awful to look at, both in the giddy height at which men work and in the terrible journeys which they make when bringing down the slate in their sleds. It is simply appalling to see that small moving speck on the high crag, passing noiselessly along a narrow grey line that looks like a mere thread, and to know that it is a man with the chance of his life dangling in his hand. As we look, the speck moves; he first crosses the straight gallery leading out from the dark cavern where he emerged, and then he sets himself against the perpendicular descent and comes down the face of the crag, carrying something behind him - at first slowly and, as it were, cautiously; then, with a swifter step, but still evidently holding back; but at the last with a wild haste that seems as if he must be overtaken and crushed to pieces by the heavy sled grinding behind him. The long swift steps seem almost to fly; the noise of the crashing slate comes nearer; now we see the man's eager face; and now we hear his panting breath; and now he draws up by the road-side - every muscle strained, every nerve alive, and every pulse throbbing with frightful force.

It is a terrible trade - and the men employed in it look wan and worn as if they were all consumptive or had heart disease. The average daily task is seven or eight of these journeys, carrying about a quarter of a ton of slate each time; the downward run occupying only a few minutes, the return climb - by another path not quite so perpendicular, where they crawl with their empty sleds on their backs, like some strange sort of beetle or fly - half an hour.

Great things used to be done in former times and the quarrymen still talk of Samuel Trimmer, who once made fifteen journies in one day, for the reward of a small percentage on the hurdle and a bottle of rum; and of Joseph Clark, a Stonethwaite man, who brought down forty-two and a half loads, or ten thousand eight hundred and eighty pounds of slate in seventeen journies, travelling seventeen miles - eight and a half up the face of the crag and the same number down at this murderous pace.

The quarrymen have small sleeping-huts among the crags and remain during the week at their work, going home only from the Saturday night to the Monday morning, which leaves scarcely too much time for the building up of a man's domestic life; but they are not a bad race, though rough and uncouth, as are all men whose business leads them to much separation from women and exclusive companionship with each other.

E. Lynn Linton: *The Lake Country*, 1864.

Boring and Blasting

The extraction and treatment of slate in southern Lakeland was described in 1843.

Far off may be heard the deep sound of the blast, as it echoes among the mountains; and upon a nearer approach, the rattling of the rubble and stones, as they tumble and leap down over the sides of the hills, the incessant clatter of the slate-rivers' hammers - "tinkling animation, noisy concussion and thundering explosions" - give to these manufactories of slate a great appearing of activity. They form, too, a very prominent object and their heaps of rubbish are a sombre appendage to the hills in which they are situated. The romantic

61

positions in which they occur will repay a visit, and more especially so if the tourist be geologically inclined; for there is a rich and extensive field laid open for investigation by the immense excavations, showing the positions of the strata, joints, lamina of depositions and the planes of cleavage . . .

The quarries are worked on the side of a hill and mostly open at the top, though some are subterraneous, resembling mines; levels or tunnels being formed to bring away the rock and rubbish and to allow the water to drain off.

The slate is detached from the rock by means of blasting, in which operation the quantity of powder used on different occasions varies considerably. All the arrangements of boring and charging having been completed, the signal for the workmen to retire is given by the vociferation of the word "fi-er" which is immediately answered by all tools being laid down and retreat being made to a place of security. When not accustomed to the occurrence, the feeling of suspense between the lighting of the fuse and the explosion is rather painful and the nervous action considerable, especially when it is known that a large quantity of powder is employed - a quantity indeed which, upon some particular occasion, may amount to a barrel.

At last the fuse hisses - bang goes the blast - the rocks vibrate - crash! crash! crash! come the huge masses down, tumbling over each other as if in play. Pieces, some tons in weight perhaps, are flung against the side of the quarry; other pieces take an upward flight and, after an aerial voyage of a few hundred feet, plough up the ground and continue bounding onward until their force is broken. It rarely happens, however, that such powerful blasts as these occur, the general charge being only a pound or two of powder; but when the rock is worked into a particular position, one such will bring down an immense quantity.

The operation of boring and blasting each large piece thrown down has then to be gone through, after which the whole is reduced, by means of sledge-hammers and wedges, to such pieces as may be conveniently carried away.

The next process is that of riving or splitting the rock into thin plates. This part of the manufacture is carried on at the outside of the quarry and requires much dexterity in the workmen; the art is, indeed, only to be acquired by an apprenticeship. The plates are then formed or dressed into slates and classed according to their size and thickness. The old classification by the workmen was London's, Country's, Tom's, Peggy's and Jerry-tom's; London's being the best and the others constituting the gradations.

Beside being applied to the purpose of roofing, slate is, by sawing, manufactured into paving for street and also for ornamental paving, chimney-pieces, cisterns, mill floors, etc. Its great recommendations are durability, elasticity and strength.

Charles M. Jopling: *Sketch of Furness and Cartmel,* 1843.

Lead for Pencils

Black lead, variously known as wad or wadd, graphite and plumbago, has been mined at Seathwaite in Borrowdale for centuries. In 1749, the mine was not without its awe-inspiring qualities.

We now entered another narrow valley, which winded thro' mountains that were totally barren, and in about an hour we arrived at *Seathwaite*, which is just under the mines and, as near as I can compute, about 10 miles distant from *Keswic*. The scene that now presented itself was the most frightful that can be conceived; we had a mountain to climb for above 700 yards in a direction nearly perpendicular that we were in doubt whether we should attempt it. However, recovering our restitution, we left our horses at a little house that stood by itself on the utmost verge of the county and approached the mountain. The precipices were surprisingly variegated with apexes, prominecies, spouting jets of water, cataracts and rivers that were precipitated from the cliffs with an alarming noisc.

One of these rivers we passed, over a wretched foot-bridge, and

63

Dungeon Ghyll

soon after began to climb.

We had not ascended far before we perceived some persons at a great distance above us who seemed to be very busy, tho' we could not distinguish what they were doing. As soon as they saw us, they hastily left their work and were running away, but by a signal made by our guide, who probably was but too well acquainted with them, they returned to the number of 18.

We came up to them after an hour of painful and laborious travelling and perceived them to be digging with mattocks and other instruments in a great heap of clay and rubbish, where mines had been formerly wrought. But tho' they were now neglected by the proprietors as affording nothing worth the search, yet these fellows could generally clear 6 or 8 shillings a day and sometimes more.

The black lead is found in heavy lumps, some of which are hard, gritty and of small value; others soft and of a fine texture. The hill in which it is found is a dirty, brittle clay, interspersed with springs and in some places shivers of the rock. The hazel grows in great plenty from the bottom to the height of above 300 yards but all the upper part is utterly barren . . .

Gentleman's Magazine Vol. XXI, February 1751.

The Black Stuff

An account, written a century later, gives a much more balanced picture of the wad mine.

The famous black-lead mine of Borrowdale will, of course, be the first object of inquiry with the traveller. It is called by the people about here the "Wad mine" but this name is equally as appropriate as the other, for . . . the substance which we improperly call black lead is in reality plumbago, a compound of carbon and iron.

The mine is in the midst of a mountain about 200 feet high and, as that part of the mine which is now being worked is near the middle of the mountain, the present entrance is on the hill-side to the left about 1000 feet from the summit. The recess is called Gillercombe and is easily distinguished from the rest of the mountain by the heaps of rubbish that nearly choke up its approaches.

The aperture by which the workmen enter descends by a flight of steps and, in order to guard the treasure contained within the proprietors have erected a strong brick building of four rooms, one of which is immediately over the entrance into the mine. This opening is secured by a trap-door and the room connected with it is called the dressing-room, for when the men enter it they strip off their customary clothes and put on their mining dresses. The men work in gangs which relieve each other every six hours, and when the hour of relief comes a steward or foreman attends in the dressing-room to see the men change their dress as they come up out of the mine. Their clothes are examined by the steward to see that no black-lead is concealed in them and when the men have dressed they leave the mine, making room for another gang who change their clothes, enter the mine and are fastened in for six hours.

When sorted and dressed, the wad or black-lead is put into casks holding about one hundred-weight each and the casks are conveyed down the mountain. This apparently difficult feat is easily performed by fixing the cask upon a light sledge with two wheels and a man who is well used to the precipitous path walks down in front of the sledge, taking care that it does not acquire too great a momentum and thus overpower him, When one cask has been safely guided in this way to the bottom, the man carries the sledge up hill again upon his shoulders and prepares for another.

About the middle of last century, the mine was opened only once in seven years and a quantity, supposed to be equal to the demand for that space of time was taken out at once. Subsequently, however, the demand became greater and the quantity obtainable at any one time became smaller, so that it was found necessary to work the mine for six or seven weeks every year.

During the time of working, the mine is guarded night and day and when a quantity deemed sufficient for one year has been taken out, the mine is secured in this manner. Besides the opening at which the men enter, there is a large horizontal one capable of admitting handcarts and wheelbarrows for the removal of the rubbish and loose earth with which the wad is enveloped, and for the flow of water from the mine. All this rubbish is at the completion of the working wheeled back into the larger entrance, to the extent of several hundred cartloads by which the water is dammed up and the mine gradually flooded. All the doors are then locked and the mine is entirely deserted until the following year.

Several shafts have been worked in the mine according to the richness of the contents but there is reason to believe the mine is gradually becoming exhausted. There was a time when the plumbago was so little valued that the neighbouring shepherds used it in large quantities for marking their sheep, and within twenty years afterwards the proprietors were getting forty shillings a pound for the wad found in one single sop or vein which yielded nearly thirty tons. A considerable portion is made up into black-lead pencils at Keswick, where there are several workshops. The process of manufacture is very simple, consisting merely of sawing up the cedar into long planks and afterwards into smaller rods, in which grooves are cut by means of a fly-wheel to the size fitted to receive the black-lead. The pieces of mineral are then cut into thin slabs and subsequently into rods; these rods are inserted in the grooves and the two halves of the case are glued together.

E.L. Blanchard: *Adam's Pocket Descriptive Guide to the Lake District*, 1852.

Water and Steam

Efficiency in 1847.

The following instance of despatch in the execution of an order is without a parallel we apprehend in the history of pencil-making and is therefore not unworthy of being chronicled. It shows how much can be accomplished in the course of even a few hours by effective machinery, convenience, and a complete establishment, in every department of the business, of expert and willing workmen.

On Thursday week, an order was received by Messrs. Banks, Forster and Co. of Keswick by the London mail, which reaches that town a little before mid-day, but as the locomotive-engine by which the letters in that place are conveyed from house to house is not upon Mr Crampton's principle, the order in question would probably not reach its destination, a distance of about one hundred and fifty yards from the post-office, much before four o'clock in the afternoon! However, be that as it may, when the order did come to hand, there was not a single pencil of the kind required - "Slate in Cedar" in stock and fifty gross were wanted in London at an early hour on Saturday morning, otherwise they would be useless.

The work was set about instanter. The unshapely pieces of stone were cut into the required scantlings; the wood was cut up and grooved to receive the pieces of slate, but before a sufficient quantity of "grooves" and slate were ready to put into the hands of the "fitters in" six o'clock had arrived. Shortly after that hour, however, the fitters in commenced their portion of the work and before three o'clock on Friday morning the whole were fitted in and glued together!

The men resumed their work at the usual hour on Friday morning and immediately commenced with the various processes of rounding, polishing, cutting into the required lengths, stamping, tying up in labelled packages of a dozen each and finally into parcels of half a gross each, the whole of which operations were gone through with perfect ease, and the fifty gross, or 7200 pencils, were despatched by the mid-day mail to Kendal, from whence they would be forwarded by the mail-train to London the same evening and thus reach the metropolis on Saturday morning, some hours before the usual hum of business was heard in the streets of that great city! So much for what can be accomplished by the extraordinary powers of water and steam! By the aid of the former, upwards of 7000 pencils are carried through their various processes in one establishment and completed within sixteen hours; and by the still more marvellous power of the latter the said pencils are conveyed from Keswick to London in the short space of fourteen hours!

Carlisle Patriot, 7 May 1847.

Making Charcoal at the Pitstead

Elsewhere men were busy deep in the woods of Furness making charcoal.

The place in the wood, called the pitring or pitstead, where the charcoal is made, is a circular clearing from twenty to thirty feet in diameter, practically level, and usually situated in a convenient and sheltered position with a supply of water close at hand. During the spring and summer, the wood is cut up, the thicker pieces into lengths of three and the others of about two feet and stacked round the pitting in readiness for coaling in the late summer and autumn. A stake is placed in the centre of the pitting and the pieces of wood are piled concentrically around it, the central pieces being almost vertical and the others gradually increasing in inclination towards the circumference. A second layer is added and the top covered with more wood laid horizontally, the whole being closely packed and the interstices filled with smaller pieces. The stack is then carefully covered with coarse grass, rushes, or similar material, called cover, and on the top of this is spread a thin layer of finely sifted marl.

The pit being now ready for firing, the stake is withdrawn and the space filled with dry wood, which is fired, and afterwards the opening is closed with a piece of turf. In about twenty-four hours, when carbonization is complete, the colliers carefully rake off the cover and make the surface of the stack quite even. A fresh covering of marl is then spread over the stack and a sprinkling or "saying" of water is thrown over it which causes steam to penetrate and effectually cool the charcoal. The sprinkling requires a certain amount of skill and nothing has been found to answer the purpose better than a shallow dish, which is referred to as a "say" as far back as 1720.

This process of charcoal burning, if properly conduced, gives a result as regards both quality and yield not surpassed by any other. It requires no permanent and little moveable plant, so that the wood can be charred at the place where it is cut and the trouble of carrying it from a distance is avoided - a most important consideration, since the wood weighs nearly five times as much as the charcoal it yields.

Alfred Fell: *The Early Iron Industry of Furness and District*, 1908.

Chapter 6: UNWILLINGLY TO SCHOOL

Esthwaite Water from the Ulverston Road

Ye Youth rejoice at this foundation
Being laid for your edification

Inscription above the door of Blencowe School, 1577.

Good Report

Speaking in 1862, Lord Brougham gave Westmorland schools of 1817 a five star commendation.

It is my bounden duty to state that forty-five years ago, when what may be called the education movement began, that celebrated committee, the Education Commission, sat in the House of Commons, of which I had the honour to be chairman; at that time we found Cumberland and Westmorland very high indeed, in point of education, in comparison with the rest of the country.

Cumberland was not so high as Westmorland. Westmorland was the highest of all England, in proportion of the schools and children going to these schools, to the population of the country. I believe there was only one country in the world, which was part of Switzerland, that exceeded Westmorland in proportion.

W. Pearson: Papers, Letters and Journals of William Pearson, 1863.

Long Days

School began early in 1789 at Cartmel.

The master in summer shall go to school at six o'clock in the morning and come to breakfast and allow one hour for breakfast and then return to school and stay till twelve noon, and go into school at two o'clock in the afternoon and stay till six o'clock in the evening; and in winter shall go into school at eight o'clock in the morning, and to have their breakfast before they come to school and stay till twelve o'clock at noon and in the afternoon shall go to school at one o'clock and stay until five in the evening; and shall only allow Saturdays for holidays and shall not keep any red letter days as holidays, except one week at Easter, a fortnight holiday at Whitsuntide and one month at Christmas.

J. Stockdale: Annals of Cartmel, 1872.

Good Behaviour

The statutes laid down by Archbishop Sandys for Hawkshead School, founded 1585, covered all aspects of school life. Here is No. 13.

That the Usher be obedient to the Master; and the scholars shall be of honest and virtuous conversation, obedient to the Master and the Usher in all things touching good Manners and Learning both in the School and elsewhere, and shall continually use the Latin Tongue or Greek Tongue within the School as they shall be able. Also they shall use no weapons in the School, as Sword, Dagger, Waster [cudgel] or other like, to fight or brawl withal, nor any unlawful gaming in the School. They shall not haunt Taverns, Alehouses, or play at any unlawful Games, as Cards, Dice, Tables, or such like.

G.M. Tweddell: *Furness Past and Present*, 1870.

Bells and Brooms

Blencowe School was endowed by Thomas Bowerbank in 1576 and rebuilt in 1795. The following rules were to be observed.

1. The Bell shall be rung by the Boys, each his own Week, in Rotation at Seven o'clock a.m. and at Half past One p.m. from Easter 'till Michaelmas. And from Michaelmas 'till Easter at a Quarter before Eight a.m. and at One p.m.
2. The Boys, all clean and washed and combed, shall be in the School within Ten Minutes after the Bell has rung or be subject to a Task or other such Punishment as the Master shall think proper to inflict.
3. Whoever breaks a Window shall immediately cause the same to be repaired at his own Faience. And if the Offender cannot be discovered, such Window shall be repaired by general Subscription of the Boys.
4. Whoever cuts his Name in any part of the Wainscot, Seats or Benches, or otherwise cuts or intentionally injures them, shall for the first Offence forfeit Two Shillings, for the Second Four Shillings,

and for the Third Five Shillings, or be expelled the School.

5. No more than One Boy shall go out at once, nor stay longer than Five Minutes.

6. All the Boys shall have Half an Hour's Liberty in the Forenoon, viz. from Ten o'clock 'till Half past Ten, or from Half past Ten 'till Eleven, as the Master shall think most convenient. At least this shall be observed during the Summer Half Year.

7. The Same Boy that has the Care of the Bell shall also sweep the School, with the assistance of the next Boy below him. And the Brooms shall be purchased by Subscription.

8. The Holidays shall be Five Weeks at Christmas, One Week at Shrovetide, Ten Days at Easter, a Month at Whitsuntide or Midsummer, and the St Days (upon Application to the Master the Evening before) as usual.

N.B. The School shall commence and conclude with a Prayer.

Teacher's Perks

Schoolmaster and clergyman needed additional means of supplementing their meagre salaries.

In Cumberland, when the village schoolmaster does not receive adequate pay to support 'imself from his scholars' quarter-pence he is allowed what is called a *whittle-gait* or the privilege of using his knife, in rotation, at the tables of those who send their children to his school, and if he be not a bashful trencherman, he never finds any reason to regret this mode of dining by rotation, as every good housewife always provides against his *whittle-day* a *cowed-lword* [a pudding of oatmeal and suet] and a piece of beef or mutton. Not many years ago, a *harden sark*, a *guse-grassing*, and a *whittle-gait* were all the salary of a clergyman; in other words, his entire stipend consisted of a shirt of coarse linen, the right of commoning geese, and the more valuable privilege of using a knife and fork at the table of his parishioners.

Ann Wheeler: *Westmorland and Cumberland Dialects*, 1839.

74

Happy Escape

The lifestyle of a schoolmaster had its compensations, as John Marshall, schoolmaster at Newlands near Keswick in 1804, discovered.

If at any time the heat of the meridian sun induced me to prefer the shade of the trees to a walk through the fields, my dinner was forwarded to me covered with a clean napkin, and a ramble of 100 yards would furnish me with a dessert: I could recline on nature's verdant carpet, sheltered by the mountain ash or venerable oak, and feast on the wild raspberry; and, in the proper season, nuts were every where to be found in profusion.

During the interval of dinner, the boys would bathe in the shallow, brook and take me with their hands a supper of excellent trout; I had no superfluities, but happily my desires were not inordinate. I lived in peace with all mankind; my vacant hours were dedicated to reading, music, tracing rivulets to their sources, and ascending the mountains; content smoothed my pillow, and uninterrupted friendship with all my neighbours sweetened each revolving day; the contemplation of rural scenery, more particularly in these Alpine regions, cannot fail to elevate the mind to the Great Author of the sublime and beautiful objects, which every where present themselves to the view.

Happy escape from a noisy and turbulent world!

J. Marshall: *The Village Pedagogue*, 1817.

Poultry and Punishment

Education, for many children, meant the Dame School. The one at Coldbeck in Ravenstonedale was typical.

The Dame was a tall, strong, and yet withal kindly woman. The number of scholars varied about twenty, sometimes more and sometimes less. School began in the morning and included boys and girls. They came provided with their dinners. Their education consisted of learning to read and spell; writing was not included in the course. The extras were hints on how to kill poultry and lectures on good manners. Every boy and girl was required to make a bow or curtsey as they entered the school and on leaving it. They were also instructed to bow or curtsey to the aged or highly-respected inhabitants of the dale when they met them on the road. To prevent any scholar from idleness whilst the school was going on, each child, boy or girl, was required to knit. The punishment inflicted by the Dame for carelessness or bad behaviour was to stand on one leg behind the door.

W. Nicholls: *The History and Traditions of Ravenstonedale,* 1914.

Young Ladies

Miss Clough's school at Eller How, Ambleside, was very different from the Dame School at Coldbeck.

The schoolroom was built at the back on a level with the upper story, and Miss Clough had the drive brought round and a flight of steps made, so that the day-scholars need not pass through the house. There were about forty of these, from the principal families around, but only two boarders, another little girl and myself; she was my only playmate and had beautiful toys. There was a particular corner in the shrubbery where we used to sit with our dolls, and in the winter we ran up and down the gravel terrace with our hoops - it was always warm there . . .

We used to read Grecian history - from a book of her brother's, I believe - for I recollect pronouncing the names Alcibiades and Thucydides as if the last two syllables were one. The dictation was what I used to like best. We had that twice a week and always in pen and ink in exercise books.

Miss Clough stood up and read one line, and as soon as all the girls were ready she read another, but never would repeat a word or a line. She used to say, "I give you so much dictation because you learn three things at a time: first, to pay attention; second, you learn to write; and third, you learn to spell. Then, when it's all over, you have something that you will never forget." . . .

Every morning at nine o'clock, she came in and we all stood round the room in rows, with a Bible in our hands, and each read a verse aloud, and that was all - no explanations; then we shut our Bibles and went to our different classes . . . On Sundays in the morning Miss Clough come to church with us. I used to like that because sometimes an uncle of mine, who lived at Dove's Nest (Mrs Hemans' old house) came over and preached and would take me back to dinner. In the afternoon we had to write out in a book the text and as much as we could remember of the sermon, and learn the Collect, and so on. In a general way, when we had nothing particular to do, she would tell us to write out the Beatitudes.

Then she was very great on examinations, which went on for a fortnight before the holidays. We had a number of blank books given us for the different subjects and she would call out the questions; we wrote each one on the top of a page and left the rest blank for the answer; two subjects were taken at the same time but only every alternate girl took the same one, so that there could be no cribbing, and Miss Clough: would march round and see that there was no conversation. Then marks were given. some for neatness though the answer might be wrong, and there were special examination prices, different from the general half-year prizes, and they were always sent to us after we had gone home.

Another of Miss Clough's ideas was that every girl ought to learn to work. I was very indignant when she told me this and said, "Ladies don't have to work; they have servants to work for them." "That's all very well," she said, "but how do you know that some day or other you may not be obliged to work? Every girl ought to learn housework and be made to do it herself, so as to know how to do it if the necessity arose." She certainly taught me to dust, for I remember her showing me in the drawing-room how to pick up each separate piece of china and

Furness Abbey South East

dust it, and then dust under it and put it back.

One Saturday she announced that I was going to learn how to starch and iron. I was handed over to Margaret, the house-maid! I watched her make some starch and dip a collar in and then lay it out; I was told to iron it but I refused, and said ladies had washerwomen to do these things; so I put my hands behind me and the iron got cold. Then I suppose Margaret fetched Miss Clough, for she told me I must be punished for being disobedient and sent me into the schoolroom to darn a large hole in an old cotton stocking which she had cut for the purpose, but I didn't mind that for I was fond of sewing - it was no punishment to me. We had sewing-class in school every afternoon, she was very particular about it; in fact, it's entirely owing to Miss Clough that I can sew so well as I do.

Although she was so strict, we liked her, because she was so perfectly just. She never broke her word nor even let us off any punishment she gave us, not a hair's-breadth; but then she never punished us unless we deserved it. She had no favourites as the governesses had and never called us stupid when we made blunders; neither would she jump to conclusions, though it might appear that a child had done something wrong when it had not, but she would inquire and make allowances. I never knew her to lose her temper, or bully, or even raise her voice so that although she was so stern and precise and never smiled, we were very fond of her. In fact, she seemed to be more like a man.

T.C. Downs: *School Days with Miss Clough,* Cornhill Magazine, June 1920.

A Good Three Half-pence Worth

For the children of Workington, education, under the patronage of the Curwen family had other priorities.

The establishment of a School on the Lancaster Plan of Education, patronised by his Majesty, also redounds highly to Mr Curwen's credit. This institution contains 220 boys under the instruction of Mr Gladders, whose assiduity and abilities as a teacher have been eminently successful. These boys, for the trifling sum of three half-pence per week each, are not only instructed in the common branches of education but in navigation, the necessary elements of mathematics geography, etc. so that within the space of three years after their introduction into the school, they will have been enabled to navigate a vessel round the world! There is also at Workington a female seminary containing 90 girls under the patronage of Mrs Curwen, who are instructed both in useful learning and in domestic economy, so as not only their minds may be improved but they may be rendered fit to perform their duties in society.,

F. Jollie: *Jollie's Cumberland Guide and Directory*, 1811.

Spare the Rod?

Mr Robert Metcalf taught at Crosby Garrett from 1820 to 1863.

He believed in a liberal use of the rod and kept a good birch one on hand. This he threw with a smack at any offender and they had to carry it back to him and receive a thrashing. If they delayed in returning the rod, the punishment was increased by additional strokes administered with the thick end. Another favourite mode of punishment was to make the offending pupil stand on one leg on a particular flag in the school, holding a heavy book in his hand. Ears were pulled and boxed for small offends and he used to talk about hanging the scholars up by their thumbs, "Reading Made Easy," Markham's "Spelling Book," Walkingame's "Arithmetic" and Lindley Murray's "Grammar" were the school books in general use. The pupils were taught to write with quill pens; steel ones were looked upon as an intolerable innovation. Mr Metcalfe was a lover of snuff and during school hours did not refrain from indulging in a pinch.

J.W. Nicholson: *Crosby Garrett, Westmorland*, 1914.

Holiday Task

The Rev. W. Nicholls of Ravenstonedale recalls an ancient custom known as "barring out."

It is near Brough Hill fair and the elder boys agree amongst themselves that the time has come to bar the master out and keep him out until he has agreed satisfactorily to the new terms of the new school year. This is whispered through the school and at break of day on the Thursday morning the big boys assemble, roll in a huge stone, which served year after year for that purpose, and then these seeming young rebels fixed their block of stone against the door, which they locked, bolted, barred and made perfectly secure. And now they were prepared for a siege. The younger scholars were on the outside to bring supplies to the youthful garrison in the shape of apples and gingerbread and toffee and such things as boys love. They are ready for the attack and the defenders of Gibraltar are not more resolute.

Yonder appears the expected foe and the cry is heard "Master is coming." He is near, he is at the door, he raps with his stick, and in angry tones exclaims, "You boys, let me in." But no; the bravest of the garrison appears at the window and a parley is held. Then the written terms are handed out:

The Articles of Ravenstonedale School

Be not surprised that these lines come to hand,
For by reading their meaning you'll soon understand;
We hope that, dear sir, you will do us no harm,
And we'll show you the cause of this rude alarm.

Long, long we have toiled in heart and in mind,
To these Rules of old Syntax we've long been confined,
Week after week we this school do attend,
To Latin and Greek our minds there to bend.

Of study we've plenty, of play scarce a bit,
So hard is our study we are forced to submit
So strict are our laws, we begin to complain,
And we hope that, dear sir, it will not be in vain.

Whilst we on our beds so profoundly did sleep.
Minerva the Great into our chambers did creep;
Her dictates so sacred in mind we still hold,
And should we disclose them, you'll think us too bold.

But Horace and Virgil and poets all say
That study's more pleasant united with play,
And the rest of this week we think is our due,
And we hope, nay, we're sure of compliant from you.

Two days at Brough Hill, we hope you'll remember,
The first of October and last of September;
And when nuts become ripe two days we require,
Or else at the outside you'll keep we desire.

At Christmas a month is always our due,
And the same must be granted at Midsummer too.
Saturday for play we always require,
When we from this dungeon with pleasure retire.

And every saint day we hope you'll grant us,
And duly to Church we'll go, if you want us.
For every new scholar we ask but a day,
Contrary to which you nothing can say.

Our Sovereign's birthday you cannot refuse,
Or else disloyal we you will accuse,
And a day at each fair our city does hold
We hope you will grant us, not thinking us bold;
But if you're repugnant to this our demand,
Resolved we are at the door you shall stand.

W. Nicholls: *The History and Traditions of Ravenstonedale*, 1914.

Violent Recreation

The long-standing border enmity between the English and the Scots inspired a youthful game.

The boys to this day have a play which they call *Scotch and English*; which is an exact picture in miniature of the raid, that is, of the *inroad* by plundering parties. The boys divide themselves into two companies under two captains who choose their men alternately. They then strip off their coats, the one party calling themselves Scots, the other English. They lay their clothes respectively all on a heap and set a stone as it were a bounder mark between the two kingdoms, exactly in the middle between their heaps of clothes. Then they begin to make incursions into each other's territories, the English beginning with this reviling expression, "Here's a leap into thy land, dry-bellied Scot". And so they plunder and steal from one another all that they can lay their hands on. But if they can take hold of any invader within their own jurisdiction, either before or after he catcheth his booty, which they call a wed (the same being a Saxon word, *waed, weda, weed*, not quite out of use, signifying *clothing*) unless he escape clear into his own province, they take him prisoner and carry him to the wed or heap of clothes, from whence he is not to remove till some of his own party break in and by swiftness of foot lay hold of the prisoner before he himself be touched by any of the adverse party; which if the adversary do, be hath rescued his man and may carry him off without molestation. And thus sometimes one party will so far prevail over the other, what with plundering and what with taking prisoners, that the other shall have nothing at all left. It is a very active and violent recreation.

G. Atkinson: *The Worthies of Westmorland*, 1849.

Bad Report

The Rev. T. Ellwood visited the school at Torver in the early 1860s: all was not well.

I went to the parish school close at hand. The master was out and that was taking place which generally does take place in schools and some other public places when every man or every boy is left to do that which is right in his own eyes; there was in short a scene of considerable uproar and considerable noise. All this subsided, however, into an intense silence when I got myself fairly inside. I asked when the master would come back, but as they didn't seem to

83

know, I first took a few observations of the school and then proceeded to ask the scholars for any information I could get. It certainly was the smallest school I had ever seen, and also as far as I remembered, from its building and equipment the worst I had ever seen. The floor was in a great measure paved with rough cobble stones. Small as it was, a boarding, made up of very rough and unsightly wood, still further contracted it. The most remarkable things about it, however, were the seating and the grate - the seats were for support "let into" the wall, and in this way, with the weight of the scholars, acted as leaves and it was, as I found out afterwards, not an unusual circumstance for the end that was in the wall to give way and for the form and scholars all to go down together.

In the way of interest the grate was the masterpiece. As I learned afterwards, the heating had originally been carried out by a hearth-fire, i.e. a fire on the hearth without any grate at all. It would have been much better to have kept the hearth-fire arrangement. Someone however who was getting a new grate, for this grate had apparently been presented to the school in its last stages, had given this grate to the school and, to make matters still worse, it had been set up by an amateur who, apparently, had had his first and, as I should hope, this, his last grate-setting job here, for he had set it in such a way that the smoke came into the school instead of going up the chimney. The master, therefore, in cold weather had the alternative of having a fire by which he was half-suffocated, or no fire, when he was equally sure to be half-starved. Under these conditions he was "out" sometimes. I certainly can bear him my willing witness that in after times, when as teacher of the Sunday school, or at times of the day school, in view of this alternative, I could very willingly have chosen to be "out" myself.

T. Ellwood: Forty-five Years in a Mountain Parish, 1908.

Chapter 7: TAMING THE IRON HORSE

Bowness from Belle Isle, Windermere

We are still threatened with the nuisance of a Railway to the Vale of Windermere - but the Terminus is now not intended to come so near Ambleside but to stop a little below Orrest Head, about a mile from Bowness. By this arrangement the opposition will in some quarters be diminished, in others not at all; for what we most dread is that after they have come so far, they will not rest there, but a new attempt will be made to carry the mischief through the whole of our beautiful district.

William Wordsworth: *Letter to an Unknown Correspondent,* 17 November 1844.

Human Freight

Ruskin was equally opposed to the proposal for a railway line from Windermere to Ambleside and had some harsh words to say to the promoters of the scheme.

But the stupid herds of modern tourists let themselves be emptied, like coals from a sack, at Windermere and Keswick. Having got there, what the new railway has to do is to shovel those who have come to Keswick, to Windermere - and shovel those who have come to Windermere, to Keswick. And what then?

After all your shrieking about what the operatives spend in drink, can't you teach them to save enough out of their year's wages to pay for a chaise and pony for a day, to drive Missus and the Baby that pleasant twenty miles, stopping when they like, to unpack the basket on a messy bank? If they can't enjoy the scenery that way, they can't any way; and all that your railroad company can do for them is only to open taverns and skittle grounds round Grassmere, which will soon then be nothing but a pool of drainage, with a beach of broken ginger beer bottles, and their minds will be no more improved by contemplating the scenery of such a lake than of Blackpool . . .

But if your motive is, on the contrary, to put twopence into your own purse, stolen between the Jerusalem and the Jericho of Keswick and Ambleside out of the poor drunken traveller's pocket; if your real object in your charitable offering is not even to lend unto the Lord by giving to the poor but to lend unto the Lord by making a dividend out of the poor; then, my pious friends, enthusiastic Ananias, pitiful Judas and sanctified Korah, I will do my best in God's name to stay your hands and stop your tongues.

Robert Somervell: *A Protest against the Extension of Railways in the Lake District*, 1876.

Poetic Protest

Wordsworth protested vehemently against the Kendal to Windermere line and its extension to Ambleside. Thomas Arnold visited him at Rydal Mount in 1844.

In the autumn of 1844, at the time when plans and prospectuses were flying about proposing the continuation of the railway from Kendal to Windermere my mother paid a morning call at Rydal Mount and I accompanied her. We were shown into the dining-room, a small apartment very plainly furnished. Presently the poet appeared, having a sheet of paper in his hand; his face was flushed and his waistcoat in disarray, as if he had been clutching at it under the stress of fervid thought. "I have been writing a sonnet," he said. After a few more words, standing up in front of the fire he recited it to us; it was the sonnet "Is there no nook of English ground secure From rash assault?" the force and intensity with which he uttered the lines breathed into his hearers a contagious fire and to this hour I recollect the precise manner and tone of his delivery more exactly than in the case of any verses I ever heard.

Thomas Arnold: Passages in a Wandering Life, 1900.

Rash Assault

The sonnet, 'On the Projected Kendal and Windermere Railway', was printed in the Morning Post on 16 October 1844.

Is then no nook of English ground secure
From rash assault? Schemes of retirement sown
In youth and 'mid the busy world kept pure
As when their earliest flowers of hope were blown,
Must perish how can they this blight endure?
And must he too the ruthless change bemoan
Who scorns a false utilitarian lure

87

'Mid his paternal fields at random thrown?
Baffle the threat, bright scene, from Orrest-head
Given to the pausing traveller's rapturous glance:
Plead for thy peace, thou beautiful romance
Of nature; and if human hearts be dead,
Speak, passing winds; ye torrents, with your strong
And constant voice, protest against the wrong.

Morning Post, 16 October 1844.

Robust Reply

R.M. Milnes, M.P. was quick to reply to Wordsworth's sonnet.

The hour may come, nay must in these our days,
When the harsh stream-ear with the cataract's shout,
Shall mingle its swift roll, and motley rout.
Of multitudes these mountain echoes raise,
And thou, the patriarch of these pleasant ways,
Canst hardly grudge that crowded streets send out,
In Sabbath glee the sons of care and doubt,
To read these scenes by light of thine own lays.
Disordered laughter and encounter rude,
The Poet's finer sense perchance may pain;
Yet many a glade and nook of solitude,
For quiet walk and thought will still remain,
Where he the poor intruders may elude
Nor lose one golden dream for all their homely gain.

Cornelia Nicholson: *A Well-Spent Life: a Memoir of
Cornelius Nicholson*, 1890.

Mayor of

Kendal 1845 - 46

88

Scenic Vandalism

The proposed extension of the railway line from Windermere to Ambleside was strongly condemned.

This little section of the Lake District of only five miles in length possesses a singular wealth of fine scenery and the distant panoramic views which its open grounds its rocky eminences and its lake shores command are quite unequalled in the district. Here, says Professor Wilson, is "the widest breadth of water, the richest foreground of wood and the most magnificent background of mountains" in Westmorland. Of the existing coach road Mrs Lynn Linton says, "There is not a more lovely bit than this throughout the entire breadth of England," and to a similar effect writes nearly every one who has described the Lake Country - Green, Gilpin, Gray, De Quincey, Miss Martineau and the rest.

This road continues through the village of Ambleside to Rydal and Grasmere and past Thirlmere to Keswick. It is truly a pleasant sight on one of the great Lancashire holidays at Whitsuntide to see the crowds of factory operatives thronging this road on foot or in the cars which are amply provided for their accommodation. The hillsides and the many footpaths give space for these crowds to spread over the country, while the convenient points of access to the lakes, along the shores of which the road winds in many picturesque curves, enable them to add a little boating to the day's pleasure. It is only those who witness it who can form an idea how much the Lake Country is enjoyed by the people of Lancashire, or can appreciate the immense value of this district as a national park to the teeming population of the north. The annual excursion to the Lakes is looked forward to and discussed for months beforehand and even the poorest put by a little money to meet the expense. To this class the proposed railway would yield no advantage whatever . . .

A more hollow pretence than that of the promoters that they wish to serve that class of the community cannot be conceived. The truth is that the line is designed entirely in the interests of a few private persons. In an advertisement inserted in the local paper, signed by the ex-chairman of the promoters, this suggestion is confirmed. He states that "the Ambleside railway is intended to develop the vast mineral wealth of the Lake District" and so "to give healthy employment to the inhabitants."

As to this "vast mineral wealth" the evidence on the two defeated Ennerdale Railway Bills proved that there were no sufficient deposits of ores in the mountains of Cumberland and Westmorland to pay for the working even if there no superadded cost of transit. However, it is a fact that one of the promoters has been concerned in unsuccessful iron mines near Grasmere. Now we don't want a railway to develop iron mines at Grasmere!

The scenery which this line would irretrievably injure is so well know that description is almost needless; but besides its woodlands, crags and rocks, its streams and waterfalls and luxuriant underground of ferns and flowers, it commands, as we have said, from the higher points what is undoubtedly the finest panorama of hill and dale in England.

Pall Mall Gazette: 9 February 1887.

Line by the Lake

A suggested line from Braithwaite to Honister roused the anger of the Rev. H.D. Rawnsley.

The public has not been warned a moment too soon and owes a debt of gratitude to Mr Greenall, Lingholme, Keswick, for having sounded the alarm. The question that the Select Committee of the House of Commons will have to decide is one of great interest not only to us who are dwellers at the Lakes but to all the thousands who crowd hither annually from sifting city and railway-haunted district to find peace and freedom from the bustle of their time. And the question simply stated is this – Are the proprietors who work a certain slate quarry up in Honister to be allowed to damage irretrievably the health, rest and pleasure ground of the whole of their fellow countrymen too come there for needed quiet and rest, in order that they - the owners - may put a few more shillings a truckload into their private pockets? And this when it can be proved that all the slate required can be carted to the train and that the public are either willing to pay the price for carting that particular slate or can get as good elsewhere. Let the slate train once roar along the western side of Derwentwater, let it once cross the lovely vale of Newlands, and Keswick as the resort of weary men in search of rest will cease to be.

Each year, these public grounds of recreation and health are narrowed and invaded by private greed installed enterprise. When will true public spirit awake and, in the best interests of its age and generations of busy England yet unborn, protest and claim State protection in a matter that concerns the state only?

The Standard, 2 February 1883.

Lakes and Locomotives

'Punch' was not slow to respond to threats to Derwentwater and Loch Lomond.

> What ho! my merry Philistines,
> Here's news and no mistake:
> They're going to run a railway round
> And spoil each pretty lake;
> And near the famous cataract
> That Southey sang of yore,
> The locomotive's noise shall drown
> The murmur of Lodore.
>
> Loch Lomand, too, shall have her train,
> And I would ask, why not -

91

There's 'naething like gude dividends"
is there, my canny Scot?
It's very well in poetry
To talk of "banks and braes,"
But we prefer another bank
That punctually pays.

Don't rave about your scenery,
What's all such trash to me?
I only care for any view
That brings in £ s d:
And if you'd know the kind of scene
That I regard with pride,
A good coal-pit's the fairest thing
Upon the country-side.

A lake's a very useless thing,
And only serves to drown
The lunatics who boat thereon;
But ta'er in pipes to town,
As reservoir for waterworks,
Some little good it yields;
If not, it should be drained and made
Remunerative fields.

Then may the merry trains run on
Until each echo wakes,
And let the locomotives scream by
Scotch and English lakes;
And as commercial travellers
Are whirled by streams and hills.
They'll sigh to think the scenery
Is charged for in the bills!

Punch, 24 February 1883.

A Plea for Motive Power

J. K. Stephen expressed similar views in light-hearted verse.

Bright summer spreads his various hue
O'er nestling vales and mountains steep,
Glad birds are singing in the blue,
In joyous chorus bleat the sheep.
But men are walking to and fro,
Are riding, driving far and near,
And nobody as yet can go
By train to Buttermere.

The sunny lake, the mountain track,
The leafy groves are little gain,
While Rydal's pleasant pathways lack
The rattle of the passing train.
But oh! what poet would not sing
That heaven-kissing rocky cone,
On whose steep side the railway king
Should set his smoky throne? . . .

Wake, England wake! 'tis now the hour
To sweep away this black disgrace –
The want of locomotive power
In so enjoyable a place.
Nature has done her part, and why
Is mightier man in his to fail?
I want to hear the porters cry

"Change here for Ennerdale!" . . .
Presumptuous nature! do not rate
Unduly high thy humble lot,
Nor vainly strive to emulate
The fame of Stephenson and Watt.

93

The beauties which thy lavish pride
Has scattered through the smiling land
Are little worth till sanctified
By man's completing hand.

J.K. Stephens: *Lapsus Calami*, 1891.

A Red Letter Day

The official opening ceremony of the Cockermouth, Keswick and Penrith Railway (CKPR) in May, 1862, was a day to remember.

On Wednesday last, with banners, music and every demonstration of joy, the sun lending its splendour to the scene the first sod was cut of the C.K.P.R. The day was a memorable one for Keswick and the enthusiasm which prevailed was such as is shown only upon great occasions, Seldom, if ever, has it been equalled there, but perhaps it may be surpassed when the first locomotive, after whirling along by the margin of Bassenthwaite lake, comes to a stand under the shadow of stupendous Skiddaw.

A railway that will connect Keswick with other parts of the world beyond its mountain framework is a link that has long been wanting in the great English railway system. Such an undertaking cannot fail to benefit the locality in many respects. Irrespective of the development of trade and the resources of the district which, as in other places, will follow as a natural consequence, the railway will afford the opportunity of visiting and enjoying that rich and beautiful scenery to many who have hitherto been debarred from doing so on account of its being totally isolated from any reasonable means of communication . . . Considering the desirability of such a project as this, there is no wonder that the inhabitants of Keswick should enter into it with spirit and give to the inaugural ceremony an *éclat* which it deserved.

The weather was favourable and at Keswick every other

94

holiday requirement is ready to hand. The shops were closed in the afternoon and the population of the town was considerably increased by the arrival of large numbers from the surrounding districts, who had all come to "see t'sod cutting". About half past twelve the market place became the centre of attraction, for here the procession was to form, and consequently the market place soon became very animated and throng. There was music for the million, and confusion and bustle and noise. The Cockermouth Volunteer Engineers, with their drum and fife band, were present, as were also a number of the "Skiddaw Greys", each member of the corps wearing a green twig in his cap. Those composed the military, and then there was the St Herbert's Lodge of Oddfellows and about a thousand little boys and girls marching in regular order and swelling the procession to a great length. There were also the band of the "Skiddaw Greys" and another drum and fife band, and there was no end to the music.

But the most remarkable feature in the procession was a number of what the bills called "genuine" navvies at the head of it. They made their appearance on the scene a few minutes before the procession started and caused much amusement. They were attired in new white slops and white poke caps with a red tassle hanging from the end, and were apparently well pleased with their appearance. One of them was selected to carry the barrow and placing it on his shoulders he headed the procession, accompanied by a man carrying the spade. In the order indicated and with bands playing and banners flying, the procession marched to Great Crosthwaite, the scene of the day's proceedings.

Carlisle Journal, 23 May 1862.

Comic Opera Collection

The Ravenglass and Eskdale Railway ("Ratty") is one of Cumbria's top tourist attractions. Here it is described in 1903 by Mary Fair, the local historian.

North of Barrow-in-Furness is a junction called Ravenglass. "Change here for the Eskdale line," calls the porter. As your ticket is for Irton Road on that line, you dismount and look around for your train. The porter collects your goods and stepping across the rails past a goods shed leads you to a tiny siding whereby is a tar-coated wooden shed, covering some extremely crookedly-laid rails, three feet in gauge. On the rails are an engine of primitive design, a van ditto, and one coach still more so. The coach is a "Composite" one, containing a guard's box, one third "smoker" and an ordinary third.

These carriages hold at a pinch four slim adults a side and are innocent alike of racks, cushions or communication cords. As, however, the pace never exceeds five miles per hour, nervous passengers need not be deterred from journeying on the line on this account, for it is quite within the bounds of safety to alight while the train is going at full speed. Behind these vehicles but not coupled to them is another passenger coach containing a first-class carriage - the Royal Saloon so to speak.

Tonight this is left behind to ease the engine's burden.

There are no porters visible but presently a guard arrives, and the engine, which has been employing its leisure in giving rides to two small boys, is coupled on ahead, and the guard, a composite official, unlocks a cupboard in the dim recesses of the shed and doles out four third-class tickets to the three others and yourself who comprise his load. He then locks up his "ticket office" and, packing you in, starts his tiny train on its perilous career up the valley. It lurches and groans and rolls along in a manner that makes you wonder way you did not invest your spare coppers in insurance tickets. You also speculate whether the bottom will fall out of the carriage, the train pull up the rails, or the whole affair topple over into the river.

Thick bracken brushes the footboards at either side, from out of which the head of an ancient Herdwick ram gazes up at the snorting, labouring engine . . . Presently, with a dislocating jerk, the train pauses dead with an abruptness that lands your portmanteau on your toes, and the stoker leisurely descends to drive a misguided ewe and lamb off the track . . . This weird express grunts its toilsome way at last into "Irton Road Station", a wooden hut with a siding whereon reposes a decaying truck filled with bricks. Here you dismount and the guard starts his comic-opera collection of relics off again on its uncertain way.

The Wide World, 19 September 1903.

Chapter 8: MISFORTUNE - MAJOR AND MINOR

Upper Reach of Ullswater

During the winter of 1819 and the early part of the winter of 1820, scarcely a Tuesday passed but a farmer or miller was robbed on his return from Penrith market, and in some instances left bleeding and senseless on the highway; for these robberies were carried into effect with every accompaniment of ruffianly violence . . . General terror pervaded the country.

J. Walker: *The History of Penrith*, 1858

Trapped on the Sands

A family tragedy occurred on the sands of Morecambe Bay in about 1750: the crossing was a hazardous undertaking.

An accident of a very melancholy nature, which nearly involved a whole family, in its catastrophe, is yet fresh in the recollection of all the neighbouring country, though it occurred nearly half a century ago. An old fisherman set out to cross the sands from Cartrnel one morning, driving in his little cart his two daughters, followed by his wife on horseback, the whole party in gala dress for a day's enjoyment at Lancaster fair. Having journeyed half-way across the sands, a thick fog suddenly arose and involved them in its darkness. The track now became obscure and whilst the travellers were anxiously endeavouring to trace it, the water began to deepen around them.

Bewildered with alarm, the poor man stopped his cart and desiring the women to remain quiet, said he would go a few steps forward and endeavour to discover his well-known marks. He accordingly went but returned no more. Distracted with apprehensions for his safety, the faithful and affectionate wife would not listen lo the prayers of her daughters to hasten on from the inevitable destruction with which the rising waters now threatened her, but wandered about the spot where she had missed her husband, calling vainly on his name till she was washed from her horse and found the same common grave with him.

The sagacity of the horse saved the lives of the young women. Perfectly petrified with grief and alarm, they lost the guidance of the animal, who, turning again into the road to Cartmel, at length brought them in safety to their homes. On the ensuing day. the bodies of the faithful old couple were found upon the sands.

Richard Warner: *A Tour through the Northern Counties*, 1802.

A Hanging Matter

A misunderstanding has disastrous consequences.

Lord William Howard of Naworth Castle is said to have consumed a great part of his time nourishing his natural severity by silent solitude. To interrupt these hours of seclusion was an offence cautiously avoided by his domestics, particularly as one intrusion has been attended with fatal effects. His Lordship was one day deeply engaged among his schoolmen or fathers, when a soldier, who had captured an unfortunate moss-trooper, burst into the apartment to acquaint his master with the circumstance and enquire what should be done with the captive. "Hang the fellow!" said Lord William, peevishly; an exclamation intended to convey no other meaning than displeasure at this intrusion upon his privacy. The servant, however, accustomed to the most implicit obedience, immediately construed this passionate expression into a command, and a few hours afterwards, when Lord William directed the prisoner to be brought before him for examination, he was told that, in compliance with his orders, the man had been long since *hanged*.

Richard Warner: A Tour through the Northern Counties, 1802.

Fire Alarm

The Holm Cultram Parish Register records an unfortunate accident.

It so happened that upon Wednesday, the eighteenth of April, 1604, one Christopher Hardon, carrying a live coal and a candle into the roof of the church to search for an iron chisel which his brother had left there, and the wind being exceedingly strong and boisterous, it chanced that the coal blew out of his hand into a daw's nest which was within the roof of the church, and forthwith kindled the same, which set the roof on fire, and within less that three hours it consumed and burned both the body of the chancel and the whole church, except the south side of the low church, and was saved by means of a stone vault.

J. Britton & E.W. Brayley: The Beauties of England and Wales, 1802.

Fatal Incident

An accident in a million at Kirkby Stephen church.

The church is extremely old and built low, and the steeple is about fifty four feet high, with four bells, the last of which was put up in 1749, at which time an unfortunate accident happened to the person who was employed to make frames in the place of those that were to be taken down. Having bought the old frames, he threw them down from the great window, but as he was dropping the last piece an old nail laid hold of his clothes and pulled him after it from the window, forty five feet high, by which his brains were dashed out, just when he had completed his work and was about returning to his family at Appleby.

N. Spencer: *The Complete English Traveller*, 1771.

Gable in Snow

Accidents on the fells have been recorded for many years - and still are all too common. There seems to be some confusion here between Wasdale and Ennerdale.

In February, 1865, Mr Charles Lennox Butler lost his life at the top of the Great Gable mountain at Wastdale. He was the second son of the Hon. C.I. Butler of Colon House near Rugby and only 24 years of age. He left the Derwenrwater Hotel, Keswick, to explore the mountains capped with snow. Few travellers dare commit themselves to such a country in such a season when there is imminent risk upon the rocks.

At Wastdale Head, he put up at Mr Ritson's and from thence made frequent excursions. He ascended Scawfell, the highest mountain in Cumberland, but losing himself on his return, remained with some shepherds all night and returned to Wastdale Head next day.

On the following morning he went out for the purpose of

ascending the Great Gable, a very steep mountain, 2925 feet high, saying in his accustomed pleasant manner, "I shall be back again in about three hours". Seeing nothing of him afterwards, Mr Ritson concluded that his young and ardent visitor had returned to the Derwentwater Hotel at Keswick. A frost of intense severity had set in a morning or two before the fatal fall; the snow was congealed in long glaciers down the ravines and the stones on which the traveller stepped were one sheet of ice.

Long absence caused Mr Bell, the proprietor of the Derwentwater Hotel, to write to farmer Ritson of Ennerdale on the subject of his visitor, who, instead of passing his leisure hours in vain and effeminate pastimes, he was well aware this enthusiastic admirer of God's stupendous works was always planning some scheme to add to his store of knowledge to be acquired in the grandest and most picturesque scenery. Mr Ritson became alarmed and with some other mountaineers started in search of their missing guest. They traced the marks of his snow-shoes to that part of the Great Gable Fell facing Wastwater and Ennerdale. On coming to a precipitous part, they lost these tracks but from the appearance of the snow it seemed that something had rolled down the mountain-side. As it was not safe for human foot to descend in this place, a retriever dog was sent down the steep and some distance below the dog halted and barked.

By a circuitous route, Mr Ritson gained the spot and there found the body of the unfortunate traveller, covered with snow, a portion only of his plaid protruding. He had, no doubt, while admiring the beautiful scenery around him, lost his footing on the slippery platform of the mountain and rolled down. When the snow had cleared away. Mr Ritson jun. and a party of dalesmen examined the scene of the fatal catastrophe and found that the unfortunate gentleman must have fallen a depth of at least 700 feet. It is the intention of the ill-fated gentleman's friends to erect a monument on the spot where the body was found.

G.K. Matthew: *The English Lakes, Peaks and Passes*, 1866.

Vale of Keswick

Storm Damage

St John's in the Vale near Keswick almost disappeared under a torrential storm on 22 August 1749.

There happened about four years ago a most dreadful storm of thunder and lightning in these parts, which bursting over the mountains, was attended with such a torrent of rain as considerably changed the face of the country and did incredible damage in the vale below . . .

In the afternoon which preceeded the storm, it was perceived to thunder and lighten incessantly beyond *Skiddaw*, one of our highest mountains. The cloud from which the tempest proceeded came at length up to the mountain but, not being high enough to pass over it, divided. One half of it went away north east and meeting with no opposition it discharged a great quantily of water on the plains of *Wigton* and *Carlisle*, over which it hovered till about nine o'clock at night and then moved farther in the same direction but so slowly that its explosions were not out of hearing till two in the morning.

The other half went through a vale called *Threkot* [Threlkeld] and over the rocks on one side of *Keswic* called *Lady Rocks*, meeting no opposition till it came to the mountains which bound *St John's* vale and by these it was stopped. It became every moment more dense by the accession of vapours, which, being still in motion, pressed upon it and soon after it poured down a torrent of rain which lasted eight hours.

The thunder still continued and the darkness, which might almost be felt, became more dreadful by the flashes which broke it at short intervals with a sulphureous light. To the noise of the thunder was added that of the cataracts and of the fragments of the rock which they drove before them. The fences (stone walls) were overturned in a moment, the fields covered with the ruins of the mountains, under which the cottages were first crushed and then swept away by the torrent.

The inhabitants, who were scarce less astonished and terrified than they would have been at the sound of the last trumpet and the dissolution of nature, ran together from under the roofs that sheltered them, lest they should be beaten in upon their heads, and finding the waters rush down all round them in an impetuous deluge which had already covered the ground, such of them as were able climbed the neighbouring trees, and others got on top of the haystacks where they lay exposed to the lightning and the rain, discovering by the light of every flash some new ruin and every moment expecting that the trees to which they had fled for safety should be torn up by the rain and the hay overturned by the inundation.

It is perhaps impossible for the strongest imagination to accumulate circumstances of greater horror and these were produced by a concurrence of various causes, which perhaps may happen no more.

Gentleman's Magazine Vol. XXIV, October 1754.

A Cataract of Thick Ink

A rare and frightening natural disaster threatened Solway Moss near Longtown.

Late in the night of Novemner 17, 1771, a farmer, who lived near the Moss, was alarmed with an unusual noise. The surface had at once given way and the black deluge was rolling towards his house. By the light of a lanthorn, he perceived the cause of his affright but thought it something preternatural. However, he had the prudence to alarm his neighbours with all expedition, though some were not waked till the Stygian tide had entered their houses; and their suspense and terror were indescribable, till the return of morn.

About three hundred acres of moss were found to be discharged and four hundred acres of arable land covered. The houses were either overthrown or filled to the roofs, yet providentially not a human life was lost.

The eruption burst from the place of its discharge like a cataract of thick ink mixed with fragments of peat. The farther it flowed, the more it expanded and lessened in depth till it reached the river Esk.

The surface of the Moss received a considerable change. What was before a plain, now sunk into a vast basin and thus afforded a view from Netherby of land and trees unseen before.

Thomas Pennant: Second Tour in Scotland, 1772.

The Solway Moss

The creeping mass continued to spread and six weeks later.

Solway Moss is still moving and it is said has now covered 900 acres of as fine holm land as there is in England. It has stopped the road for these eight days past betwixt Annan and Longtown and the post is obliged to boat over the river Esk.

Gentleman's Magazine Vol. XLII, January 1772.

Passionate Intrigue

Completely different was what might be called the case of Jonathan Sewell versus Ann Heslop, Thomas Wallis, Thomas Leek, John Wilson, another man called Wilson, and Bousted.

A widow named Ann Heslop resided at Stanwix near Carlisle and Jonathan Sewell, a considerable landowner, resided at Durdar. Sewell was commonly known as "The Laird". He was a simple man, much addicted to liquor, and seventy years of age. When in liquor he expressed great affection for the widow but at no other time was he troubled with the tender passion.

Assisted by her friends, the widow made two unsuccessful attempts to get married to him when drunk. Thus foiled she applied to Wallis, who undertook the business in consideration that he was to be liberally rewarded if he succeeded in consummating the wished for event.

On the 13th of September, 1788, Sewell was carried off in a post chaise, from a harvest field on his own estate, having first been induced to drink till he was intoxicated, and conveyed to Penrith by Wallis, Thomas Leek, Wilson, John Wilson and the widow. From Penrith, the old man was removed for safe keeping to . . . Stanhope in Weardale and thence back to Penrith to Wallis's house where he was confined in the uppermost story tor thirty-six weeks. The windows were nailed up with boards and one of Wallis's servants attended him as keeper, day and night. A writ of Habeas Corpus - the great writ of English liberty - in which Leek, Wilson and other parties suspected of being concerned in his detention were included, was served on Waliis on the 24th October, but disregarded, for Wallis was resolved not to give up his prisoner until he could hand him over in marriage to the widow. But all his designs were thwarted by one little incident. One of his servants - a lad about 18 years of age - left at Martinmas, 1788, and being threatened by Sewell's friends, he disclosed all he knew of the matter, conducted them to the place of Sewell's confinement and the poor old

106

imbecile was forthwith released from his long captivity.

At the Assizes held at Carlisle on the 15th of August, 1789, Wallis, the widow Heslop, Leek, Wilson, John Wilson and Boustead, the widow's brother, were indicted for conspiracy, convicted and sentenced to various terms of imprisonment which they respectively underwent. Wallis's punishment was the most severe. He was three times exhibited in the pillory and imprisoned for three years.

J. Walker: *The History of Penrith*, 1858.

Battle at Bootle

In 1838 the peace of a small Cumbrian village was shattered by a battle.

On Saturday, August 18, 1838, early in the morning, a most sanguinary conflict took place at Annaside. near Bootle, Cumberland, between the inhabitants of that hitherto peaceful village and the crews of three vessels, assisted by a number of persons from Ravenglass under the command of a leader named Wilson, who was an innkeeper there.

It appears that a practice had grown up for vessels to load cobbles from the sea shore and in consequence of this removal the tide was making inroads on the land, the parish having been put to considerable expense, so that it was resolved that a stop should be put to it. Despite all protests, however, Wilson continued to load vessels for Runcorn and Liverpool with the cobbles. So, as peaceful means failed, the inhabitants determined to try force.

Having removed all the stones from Stub Place, Wilson on Friday began to load three vessels from the beach, when the villagers drove them to their vessels. Next morning, Wilson brought up a strong reinforcement of both sexes, himself armed with a huge pump handle and his followers with spars and bludgeons. On seeing this, there was an assembly from Whitbeck and Bootle to assist Annaside, in all some thirty-six men, each carrying a good sprig of oak.

A most desperate fight ensued, the women pouring in volleys of stones in addition to the noise they made. In the thick of the fight Wilson signalized himself by a desperate attempt to give a finisher to Mr Parker with his formidable weapon, but this circumstance attracted notice and his sconce was made to crack again by the repeated blows inflicted upon it by the oaken weapons of his antagonists.

With the fall of Wilson, the battle was over and the villagers victorious. There were many contusions but happily none slain. Men were to be seen at the close of the combat lying in all directions with broken heads and bruised bodies; one man had his leg fractured and numbers on both sides were so severely injured that they had to be conveyed home, and are as yet confined to their beds - some of them, it is asserted, are in a dangerous state.

The women finally effected their purpose and drove the enemy to their ships. The language of the women was said to be frightful. When the tide served, the vessels went to Ravenglass and so ended the "Battle of Annaside".

Whitehaven News.

Chapter 9: OVER THE HILLS

Crummock and Buttermere Lakes

*The country, your companions and the length of your journey
will afford a hundred compensations for your toil.*

Ovid (43BC - AD17)

Why Walk?

Two feet are better than four wheels.

One of the many advantages of being a pedestrian is that, if there be half a dozen ways of visiting a mountain or a mere, you can take which way you like best. He who travels in his carriage requires a broad road, and he who rides on horseback is stopped at once by a fall or a bog, or a fastened gate, or a stile, or a fence, whereas a pedestrian easily overcomes all these obstacles. Give me then health, cheerfulness and a walking-stick; and you, if you prefer it, may travel in a coach and six.

George Mogridge: *Loiterings among the Lakes of Cumberland and Westmorland*, 1849.

Delights of Buttermere

Fell walking is much more than merely putting one foot in front of the other.

The most agreeable way of employing a few days at Buttermere is to roam over and among the wild hills and deep glens in its neighbourhood; this, to me, is an amusement so incomparable to the mere cut-and-dried road travelling, that I have ever used the opportunity, when it offers, of indulging in such humour freely: and to those who have never tasted its pleasurable excitement and release from all constraint, it cannot be understood - but, once partaken of, it will most assuredly be tried again and again by every tourist fond of the wild and untrammelled beauties of nature.

Let but the uninitiated imagine tor one moment, the pleasure of flying for a brief space from the busy haunts of men, to dive deep into the wild solitude of the hills, to climb each rock and crag with the buoyancy of health and life (which the pure and invigorative air alone properly sustains), to pace with brisker motion along the velvety and sweet-smelling heather that starts elastic from beneath the foot that

110

presses it, as if to give renewed activity and vigour to the whole frame - making the blood course merrily through the veins and arteries of the self-elated man, as if it would burst the trammels that confine it; and then to watch the mimic cataracts, as they come tumbling and rolling down the steep sides of the mountains, meeting in little hollows, where, bubbling and frothing for a brief moment, as if in anger at each other's company, the tiny streams, in blissful union met, flow on as one to some far deeper level, where, with calmer peace and wider current, brushing the wild flowers with its fresh and moistening touch, it disappears behind some huge projecting buttress, to unite its waters with that of the vale below.

In the free use of such enjoyment, I have spent many a summer day, rambling about each hill and dale, with no other company than my thoughts - and no other indicator of my whereabouts than the great orb of light; and, in all these rural journeys, I have received most manifest proofs that it is not unwholesome to the body, whatever it may be to the mind.

J. Onwhyn: *Pocket Guide to the Lakes*, 1841.

Scaling the Pikes

Writing in 1836, George Tattersall recommends the Langdale Pike.

I would recommend the ascent of this mountain-summit to the notice of the tourist for two reasons: in the first place, the intrinsic beauty of the surrounding scenery will amply repay him tor the trouble; and moreover, because in ascending this the first of the major mountains, he sees the field of his future operations spread out far before him, and he is thus enabled to become better acquainted with the ground which he is about to traverse, and with the most striking objects and land-marks on his future way.

The ascent of the Langdale Pikes is not very difficult: but it is yet sufficiently steep to prepare the pedestrian for the more arduous ascents of Helvellyn and Skiddaw; many of the fair sex have, however, graced the rough summit of Harrison Stickle.

And here I must be allowed a moment's digression, in order to give a few short words of advice to the pedestrian tourist, relative to his equipment. For mountain-climbing, shoes and gaiters will be found to be at once more serviceable and agreeable than boots; a long staff, armed at one end with an iron spike, will also be of great use and assistance; and a small flask of weak brandy and water will not be deemed ungrateful by the thirsty aspirant; a linen jacket and a light cap or straw-hat will complete his equipment and he is then, to use the *patois* of the country "in good fettle to clim' t'fells."

George Tattersall: The Lakes of England, 1836.

Safari to Fairfield

Are we to take James Payn's "tremendous ascent" of Fairfield seriously?

Fairfield is about 3,000 feet above the level of the sea; and we proposed to sleep upon the summit of its huge green back. The news spread like wild-fire through the little village; offers of service poured in from every quarter - guides, lanterns (even a boat from one person, who thought it would be a very snug affair turned upside down), ponies, mules - camels would, I doubt not, have been forthcoming, had we desired them - everything we wanted, and many things of which we had no need, were pressed upon us eagerly.

We had already an alpenstock apiece (which for my own part, since it is for ever getting between my legs and tripping me up, 1 do not consider an assistance), and a railway-rug; and the landlord of our hotel provided the provisions. These were the chief of the necessaries which my sagacity procured for our night-time bivouac and tremendous ascent: thirty-six bottles of bitter beer, two bottles of gin, two bottles of sherry, one gallon of water, four loaves of bread, one leg of lamb, one leg of mutton, two fowls, one tongue, half-pound of cigars, four carriage-lamps, and two packs of playing-cards. We had also a large tent, which was carried on the back of a horse. Three men were necessary to pitch this tabernacle and to carry the provisions.

About five o'clock in the afternoon we started for the mountain with a huge train of admirers, forming the largest cavalcade that had ever left Ambleside before.

James Payn: *Leaves from Lakeland*, n.d.

Dread Suspense and Dire Foreboding

A foreign visitor is rescued from the brink of a precipice.

In the month of July 1847, a party from Manchester, amongst whom was a foreigner, commenced the ascent of the Langdale Pikes and when about half the distance, this gentleman, feeling fatigued, agreed to rest himself till the return of his comrades. Observing the clouds touching the mountain tops and thinking his friends might have miscalculated their return, he began to retrace his steps, as he thought in the right direction, but soon found the brow of the mountain becoming steeper, and at last came to the brink of a precipice nearly forty yards high.

He still thought it might be possible to descend gradually by the help of a tree growing out of the rock, and to aid in his descent, he stripped, look off his shirt, cut it up into shreds which he tied together, fastened to the tree and, after weighing the chances of danger as to going down or up, he deliberately chose the former as the safer of the two courses, and lowered himself down to a ledge a good number of feet below the edge! But when there, he saw the impossibility of further progress either way.

It was now about seven o'clock; the clouds were descending the mountains and his situation had become most alarming. He endeavoured io attract attention by shouting and waving his vest and handkerchief, though neither house nor person was in sight. His strength gradually gave way under the exertion and long-continued excitement. His footing was as nothing and he was, from his situation, incapable of moving.

Most providentially, his alarm had been heard in the vale below and his signs observed. After a long interval of dread suspense and dire foreboding, he had the unspeakable pleasure of observing at a great distance below him, six figures wending their way up a distant shoulder of the hill. Their steps seemed directed towards him, and soon he became sure of this, as he observed they carried a something which he could not at first make out: this turned out to be a large coil of rope. One of the six was let down by his fellows, with a rope round his body. He fastened an end round the almost sinking wanderer and he was immediately hoisted up in safety and conducted by his deliverers to the farm-house, where the greatest attention was paid him by the good people there.

James Payn: *A Hand-Book to the English Lakes*, n.d.

Boggy Bewilderments

Edwin Waugh gets into difficulties crossing from Buttermere to Wasdale in 1860.

Gatesgarth is a large farmstead, a little beyond Buttermere, and at the foot of Honister Crag. Seen from this spot, that mighty amphitheatre of precipitous rock is a grand sight. At Gatesgarth guides may be had. The day was getting far spent when we arrived there and I had the old Ennerdale landlady's advice in my mind about losing our way. But there was not a guide at home. The last had gone with a man to Wastdale some time before; and the girl said we should very likely meet him.

The toughest part of the journey was still before us and there was nothing for it but to start to work. As we toiled up Scarf Gap, Honister

Crag grew ever more awfully impressive. Its frowning solitude was more widely and distinctly under the eye. marked with wandering streaks of white, where the waters came down from wilderness too savage for anything but storm and cloud to abide. We panted up. The last nook of Buttermere glided out of sight and the valley disappeared.

Higher yet we climbed and twined among scattered rocks, whilst on each hand steep crags glared silently down through the mist. On the crown of the pass, we came to a little platform of swampy land where the track grew faint and began to branch off this way and that, always ending in impassable bog or in some untrodden part of the solitude. The wind blew wild and chill and great clouds of thick mist folded us so completely in their damp embrace that we were getting wet through and at times could hardly see a yard in front of us.

At last we caught sight of the path disappearing upon the edge of the mountain; and we rattled down the glen through which the river Liza runs from Great Gable to Ennerdale Water. A tall young shepherd was coming up the mountain, with a plaid on his shoulder and a long staff in his hand. This was the guide of whom they spake at Gatesgarth. I was inclined to take him to Ennerdale with us but my friend put a good face on the matter and thought we should manage very well. The guide pointed to a solitary little tree up the glen and near the foot of Black Sail, telling us that we should find the path to Wastdale on the side of it.

It seemed easy enough to get there, so we set off again with a will, not thinking of the mosses, waters, slaps and boggy bewilderments that lay between us and our mark. Down we went over rocks, shingles and "slape places"; and through spongy, deceitful spots where lurking waters made the mountain green with swamp verdure. In the hollow, our path was dim, splashy and erratic. At last we came to a ruined cottage, nearly opposite the tree before mentioned. Here we lost the path again and found also that the river Liza was between us and Black Sail. Whichever way we turned, the swamp began to swallow us as if it were hungry.

Lower Fall at Rydal

Night was coming on; fits of heavy rain began to fall and mist-laden winds raged savagely around as if they were glad to catch us in such a place at such a time. Dashing recklessly through the swamp, we waded the stream and clambered over the rocks as straight as possible to the tree. We drew near it and looked about, but the dark steep seemed pathless. We went nearer and, to our delight, perceived a narrow path about a hundred yards to the right of the tree. If we could keep this track, there would just he about enough daylight to see us over the mountain. We found this pass wilder than Scarf Gap but we worked in that howling storm up to the top, when the rain ceased and we felt comparatively comfortable.

After our difficulties that wild October nightfall, I was not much surprised to find that "Black's Guide" calls this route to Wastdale "so perplexing that although the hardy pedestrian, with very minute directions, might succeed in finding his way over the mountains; yet everyone who has crossed them will be aware of the danger of the attempt and the fatal consequences attending a diversion from the right path."

Edwin Waugh: Rambles in the Lake Country, 1861.

Danger on Helvellyn

A famous scientist averts a disaster.

On a fixed day in every June for between thirty and forty years, a grave gentleman, the lines of whose calm, philosophic countenance scarcely showed the deepened pencillings of age from one season to another, might be seen climbing the steep sides of the mountain with a step so elastic that it distanced even old Matthew Jobson, his annual guide - mine host of the Nag's Head at Wythburn. Sometimes there is a group of friends in attendance, but, no, *they* can't keep up with the quiet old gentleman in whose face an unwonted enthusiasm breaks out in gleams. Ah! *that* too is one of the beautiful accidents of mountain atmosphere.

"John, I wonder what thy legs are made of," exclaims one of his toiling brethren behind him. This "John" is no less man than the celebrated philosopher, Dr Dalton. He says he climbs Helvellyn every year "to bring into exercise a set of muscles which would otherwise have grown stiff."

But there are other motives, for there is a whole array of instruments, apparently for making meteorological observations, and a set of little labelled bottles into which he requests those winds to breathe which dwell in the caves of the mountain and sport about its brow. The bottles were carried up full of water, which was poured out at different altitudes on their progress and, of course, the air immediately took its place. These corked-up breezes are for future analysis.

The writer knew the unassuming old philosopher in his plain strength, his serene simplicity, with which his sober garb as one of the Society of Friends harmonized well. On one of his thirty or forty ascents of Helvellyn, he and his companions suddenly found themselves enveloped in a dense cloud which had swept up and closed around them unawares. They attempted to move and stepped a few feet in advance, holding by the skirts of each other's coat, when the old philosopher suddenly drew back, saying, "Not a step more: there is nothing but mist to tread on." It was true; their unconscious feet were on the very edge of the precipice which plunges sheer down to the Red Tarn.

William Palmer: *Tales of the Mists: Gentleman's Magazine, 1901.*

A Classic Ascent

In June, 1886, W.P. Haskett-Smith climbed Napes Needle - a first ascent often regarded as the beginnings of rock climbing as a sport in Britain.

One day in the early eighties, the weather was beginning to clear after two or three days of southerly gale. Masses of cloud surged up the valley, but after a forenoon of heavy rain were driven from the centre of the dale and clung tightly to the sides of the hills. After luncheon, we ventured on a walk to the neighbourhood of Piers Ghyll . . . As we mounted into the great recess of Greta Force, we were almost free from the drift and even got an occasional gleam of sunshine, but across the path to Sty Head only the lower screes were visible and Great Gable was completely concealed. Suddenly, however, the mist grew thinner and it became just possible to locate the Napes. Then they were swallowed up again, but a moment later the outermost curtain of mist seemed to be drawn aside and one of the fitful gleams of sunshine fell on a slender pinnacle of rock, standing out against the background of cloud without a sign of any other rock near it and appearing to shoot up for 200-300 feet.

The vision did not last more than a minute or two and we all thought our eyes had been tricked, as indeed to a certain extent they had been, but resolved to take an early opportunity of hunting down the mysterious rock . . .

(The chance to climb the rock came a year or two later, in June 1886)

I forgot my headache and began to examine the Needle itself. A deep crack offered a very obvious route for the first stage, but the middle portion of this crack was decidedly difficult, being at the same time blocked with stones and turf. . .

From the top of the crack there is no trouble to reach the shoulder, whence the final stage may be studied at ease. The summit is near, being, as they say in transatlantic cities, "only two blocks away" but those same blocks are set one upon the other and the stability of the top one looks very doubtful. My first care was to get two or three stones and test the flatness of the summit by seeing whether anything thrown-up could be induced to lodge. If it did, that would be an indication of a moderately flat top and would hold out hopes of the edge being found not too much rounded to afford a good grip for the fingers. Out of three missiles one consented to stay and thereby encouraged me to start, feeling as small as a mouse climbing a milestone.

Between the upper and lower blocks, about five feet up, there is a ragged horizontal chink large enough to admit the toes, but the trouble is to raise the body without intermediate footholds. It seemed best to work up at the extreme right where the corner projects a little, though the fact that you are hanging over the deep gap makes it rather a "nervy" proceeding. For anyone in a standing position at the corner, it is easy to shuffle the feet sideways to the other end of the chink, where it is found that the side of the top block facing outwards is decidedly less vertical. Moreover, at fhe foot of this side there appeared to my great joy a protuberance which, being covered with a lichenous growth, looked as if it might prove slippery, but was placed in the precise spot where it would lie most useful in shortening the formidable stretch up to the top edge.

Gently and cautiously transferring my weight, 1 reached up with my right hand and at last was able to feel the edge and prove it to be, not smooth and rounded as it might have been, but a flat and satisfactory grip. My first thought on reaching the top was one of regret that my friends should have missed by a few hours such a day's climbing, three new things and all good: my next was one of wonder whether getting down again would not prove far more awkward than getting up!

Hanging by the hands and feeling with the toes for the protuberance provided an anxious moment, but the rest went easily enough, though it must be confessed that it was an undoubted satisfaction to stand once more on solid ground below and look up at my handkerchief fluttering in the breeze.

W.P. Haskett Smith: *The First Ascent of Napes Needle: Journal of the Fell and Rock Climbing Club of the English Lake District, Vol III No. 2*, 1914.

Chapter 10: PROUD SKIDDAW

Bassenthwaite Lake

Once more I see thee, Skiddaw! once again
Behold thee in thy majesty serene,
Where like the bulwark of this favoured plain,
Alone thou standest, monarch of the scene.
Thou glorious Mountain, on whose ample breast
The sunbeams love to play, the vapours love to rest.

Robert Southey: *Proem to the Poet's Pilgrimage, 1816*

A Sort of Emulation

Skiddaw, at just over 3000 feet and within easy reach of Keswick, earns a mention in Camden's "Britannia" (1586). Across the Solway is Criffel (Scruffel).

The Skiddaw I mentioned mounts up almost to the clouds with its two tops like another Parnassus, and views Scruffel, a mountain of Anandal in Scotland, with a soul of emulation. From the clouds rising up or falling upon these two mountains, the inhabitants judge of the weather and have this rhyme common amongst them:

> *If Skiddaw hath a cap,*
> *Scruffel wots full well of that.*

As also of the height of this and two other mountains in those parts:

> *Skiddaw, Lanvellin and Casticand,*
> *Are the highest hills in all England.*

William Camden: *Britannia,* 1586.

The Place of Delight

Michael Drayton's "Poly-Olbion" (c.1620) is rather more effusive.

> When of the Cumbrian hills, proud Skiddaw that doth show
> The high'st, respecting whom, the others be but low,
> Perceiving with the floods and forests, how it fared
> And all their several tales substantially had heard,
> And of the mountain kind, as of all others he
> Most like Parnassus-self that is supposed to be,
> Having a double head, as hath that sacred mount,
> Which those nine sacred nymphs held in so high account,
> Bethinketh of himself what he might justly say,

When to them all, he thus his beauties doth display:
"The rough Hibernian sea I proudly overlook,
Amongst the scattered rocks, and there is not a nook
But from my glorious height into its depths I pry,
Great hills far under me but as my pages lie;
And when my helm of clouds upon my head I take,
At very sight thereof, immediately I make
Th' inhabitants about tempestuous storms to fear,
And for fair weather look, when as my top is clear;
Great Furness mighty Fells I on my south survey;
So likewise on the north, Albania makes me way,
Her countries to behold, when Scurfel from the sky,
That Anandale doth crown, with a most amorous eye
Salutes me every day, or at my pride looks grim.
Oft threatening me with with clouds, as I oft threatening him:
So likewise to the east, that row of mountains tall.
Which we our English Alps may very aptly call,
That Scotland here with us, and England do divide,
As those, whence we them name, upon the other side,
Do Italy and France, these mountains here of ours,
That look far off like clouds, shaped with embattled towers,
Much envy my estate, and somewhat higher be,
By lifting up their heads to stare and gaze at me.
Clear Derwent dancing on, I look at from above,
As some enamoured youth, being deeply struck in love,
His mistress doth behold and every beauty notes;
Who as she to her fall, through fells and valley floats,
Oft lifts her limber self above her banks to view
How my brave bi-cleft top, doth still her course pursue.
O all ye topic gods that do inhabit here.
To whom the Romans did those ancient altars rear,
Oft found upon those hills, now sunk into the soils
Which they for trophies left of their victorious spoils,

Ye Genii of these floods, these mountains and these dales.
That with poor shepherds' pipes and harmless herdsmen's tales
Have often pleased been, still guard me day and night,
And hold me Skiddaw still, the place of your delight."

Michael Drayton: Poly-Olbion c.1620.

Prodigious

Arthur Young, in 1768, liked the view from the top of Skiddaw.

We took our leave of this enchanting region of landscape by scaling the formidable walls of Skiddaw himself: it is five miles to the top but the immensity of the view fully repays for the labour of gaining it. You look upon the lake, which here appears no more than a little basin and its islands but as so many spots; it is surrounded by a prodigious range of rocks and mountains, wild as the waves, sublimely romantic. These dreadful sweeps, the work of nature in the most violent of her moments, are the most striking objects seen from Skiddaw; but in mere extent the view is prodigious. You see the hills in Scotland plainly; you view a fine reach of sea; command the Isle of Man; and see part of an object which I take to be an highland in Ireland, besides prodigious tracks of adjacent country.

Arthur Young: A Six Months' Tour through the North of England, 1770.

Storm Clouds

William Hutchinson, in the 1770s, experienced Skiddaw's notorious weather.

The air was remarkably sharp and thin, compared with that in the valley, and respiration seemed to be performed with a kind of asthmatic oppression . . . Whilst we remained upon the mountain, over the hills which lay between Keswick and Cockermouth, dense and dark vapours

124

began to arise, and in a little time, as they advanced upon a south-west wind, concealed those heights we had viewed half an hour before clear and distinct. Our guide was very earnest with us to quit the mountain, as he prognosticated the hazard of being wet and of losing our way in the heavy vapour from a storm then collecting, which he informed us would soon cover Skiddaw; the circumstance was too singular to be left by people curious in their observations on natural events. The clouds advanced with accelerated speed; a hollow blast sounded amongst the hills and dells which lay below and seemed to fly from the approaching darkness; the vapour rolled down the opposite valley of Newland and appeared to tumble in mighty sheets and volumes from the brow of each mountain into the vale of Keswick and over the lakes . . . Whilst we admired this phenomenon, the clouds below us gradually ascended and we soon found the summit of Skiddaw totally surrounded, whilst we on every side looked down upon an angry and impetuous sea heaving its billows. We were rejoicing in this grand spectacle of nature and thinking ourselves fortunate in having beheld so extraordinary an event, when, to our astonishment and confusion, a violent burst of thunder, engendered in the vapour below, stunned our sense, being repeated from every rock and down every dell; at the same time, from the agitation of the air, the mountain seemed to tremble; at the explosion, the clouds were instantaneously illuminated, and from innumerable chasms sent forth streams of lightning; we had nowhere to fly for safety, no place to cover our heads. To descend was to rush into the inflammable vapour from whence our perils proceeded; to stay was equally hazardous, for now the clouds, which had received such a concussion from the thunder, ascended higher and higher, enveloping the whole mountain and letting fall a heavy shower of rain. We thought ourselves happy even under this circumstance to perceive the storm turning north-west and to hear the next clap burst in the plain beyond Bassenthwaite-water.

The echoes from the mountains which bordered Keswick lake, from Newland, Borrowdale and Lodore, were noble and gave a

125

repetition of the thunderclaps distinctly, though distant, after an intermission of several seconds of tremendous silence . . . The rain, which still increased, formed innumerable streams and cascades, which rushed from the crown of Skiddaw, Saddleback and Causey-pike with a mighty noise; but we were deprived of the beauty of these water-falls by the intercepting vapour, which was not to be penetrated by the eye more than a few yards before us.

William Hutchinson: *An Excursion to the Lakes in Westmorland and Cumberland*, 1776.

A Fine Creature

Charles Lamb visited Coleridge at Greta Hall in Keswick in 1801. He climbed Skiddaw but preferred the streets of London to the fells of Cumberland.

I set out with Mary to Keswick, without giving Coleridge any notice; for my time being precious did not admit of it. He received us with all the hospitality in the world and gave up his time to show us all the wonders of the country. He dwells upon a small hill by the side of Keswick, in a comfortable house, quite enveloped on all sides by a net of mountains: great floundering bears and monsters they seemed, all couchant and asleep. We got in in the evening, travelling in a post-chaise from Penrith in the midst of a gorgeous sunshine, which transmuted all the mountains into colours, purple, etc. etc. We thought we had got into fairyland. But that went off (as it never came again -while we stayed we had no more fine sunsets); and we entered Coleridge's comfortable study just in the dusk, when the mountains were all dark with clouds upon their heads. Such an impression I never received from objects of sight before nor do I suppose I can ever again. Glorious creatures, fine old fellows, Skiddaw, etc. I never shall forget ye, how ye lay that night, like an entrenchment, gone to bed as it seemed for the night, but promising that ye were to be seen in the morning . . .

126

Derwent Water from Castle Head

We have clambered up to the top of Skiddaw, and I have waded up the bed of Lodore. In fine, I have satisfied myself that there is such a thing as that which tourists call *romantic*, which I very much suspected before: they make such a spluttering about it and toss their splendid epithets around them till they give as dim a light as at four o'clock next morning the lamps do after an illumination. Mary was excessively tired when she got about halfway up Skiddaw, but we came to a cold rill (than which nothing can be imagined more cold, running over cold stones) and with the reinforcement of a draught of cold water she surmounted it most manfully.

Oh, its fine black head and the bleak air atop of it, with a prospect of mountains all about and about making you giddy, and then Scotland afar off and the border countries so famous in song and ballad! It was a day that will stand out, like a mountain, I am sure, in my life. But I am returned (I have now been come home near three weeks - I was a month

127

out) and you cannot conceive the degradation I felt at first, from being accustomed to wander free as air among the mountains, and bathe in rivers without being controlled by anyone, to come home and work. I felt very *little*. I had been dreaming I was a very great man. But that is going off and I find I shall conform in time to that state of life to which it has pleased God to call me. Besides, after all, Fleet Street and the Strand are better places to live in for good and all than among Skiddaw. Still, I turn back to those great places where I wandered about, participating in their greatness. After all, I could not *live* on Skiddaw. I could spend a year - two, three years - among them, but I must have a prospect of seeing Fleet Street at the end of that time or I should mope and pine away, I know. Still, Skiddaw is a One creature.

Charles Lamb, 1801.

A Rum Ascent

John Keats visited the Lakes in 1818 and on 29 June wrote to his brother:

We went to bed rather fatigued, but not so much so as to hinder us getting up this morning to mount Skiddaw. It promised all along to be fair and we fagged and tugged nearly to the top, when, at half-past six, there came a mist upon us and shut out the view; we did not, however, lose anything by it: we were high enough without mist to see the coast of Scotland, the Irish Sea, the hills beyond Lancaster, and nearly all the larger ones of Cumberland and Westmorland, particularly Helvellyn and Scawfell. It grew colder and colder as we ascended and we were glad, at about three parts of the way, to taste a little rum which the Guide brought with him, mixed, mind ye, with mountain water. I took two glasses going and one returning. It is about six miles from where I am writing to the top. So we have walked ten miles before breakfast today. We went up with two others, very good sort of fellows; all felt, on arising into the cold air, that same elevation which a cold bath gives one. I felt as if I were going to a Tournament.

John Keats, 1819 .

An Upwardly Mobile Youngster

John Ruskin visited the Lakes in 1830 and recorded the tour in a poem of 2310 lines, of which 402 describe his climb of Skiddaw. He was eleven years old.

When the summit of Skiddaw was once in our view,
Through all opposition resistless we flew!
So headlong we dashed to the heart of the bog -
Our horses we spur and horses we flog,
And splashing and dashing we floundered about -
We got easily in, and not easily out!
We thought, in the quag, that we fairly were stuck,
So tenacious, so deep, and so yielding the muck! . . .
And now the steep hill being mounted, we came,
And much to our joy, to a fine, turfy plain.
The grass was so rich and its hue was so bright,
Like circles where fairies have danced through the night.
How swiftly and lightly our palfreys swept o'er,
And how swiftly and lightly our palfreys us bore,
Till we came to a spring which with gurgling sound
And bubbling and dancing sprung up from the ground.
There stay we our steeds, that we all might survey
The beautiful prospect before us which lay ...
Thus the beautiful prospect we all did survey,
Then began to prepare for the rest of the way.
Some sandwiches take and some brandy we sip,
Applying it just to the tip of the lip,
And our spirits revived and restored our strength.
We set off on the rest of our journey at length . . .
A ridge we beheld ('twas of loose, slatey stone);
It led to the summit we'd wished for so long.
But now our teeth chattered, and our noses looked blue
And our ears were assuming a Tyrian hue

For the wind, I should say that he blew from the east,
And that is an icyish quarter at best;
I mean it is cold whenever it blows,
But now it had taken such hold of our nose . . .
So struggling we forced o'er the ridge of loose stone,
Every second we thought we should over be blown;
And although of its force we did loudly complain,
The summit of Skiddaw at last we attain.
Then our swift, eager eyes we impatiently threw
On th' extensive, the wondrous, the beautiful view.

John Ruskin: *Iteriad, or Three Weeks among the Lakes.*

Next Door to Heaven

It is not surprising that Robert Southey, who lived for forty years in the shadow of Skiddaw, wrote a number of tributes to the mountain. Here he writes to his friend, Charles Danvers, in October 1803.

Yesterday with Coleridge to the top of Skiddaw, the work of four and a half hours, that is, there and back; but the descent is mere play. Up hill a man's wind would fail him, though his lungs were as capacious as a church-organ, and legs would ache though the calves were full-grown bulls.

The panorama from the summit is very grand . . . The summit is covered with loose stones split by the frosts, and thus gradually they are reduced to a very rich soil, and washed down to the glens, so that, like old women, Skiddaw must grow shorter. For some distance below, nothing but moss grows - for it is bleak up there, next door to heaven.

John Wood Warter: *Selections from the Letters of Robert Southey*, 1856.

Celebration

On Monday, 21 August 1815, Southey and his friends celebrated Waterloo on the top of Skiddaw. Two days later he wrote to his brother, Harry.

Monday, the 21st of August, was not a more remarkable day in your life than it was in that of my neighbour Skiddaw, who is a much older personage. The weather served for our bonfire, and never, I believe, was such an assemblage upon such a spot. To my utter astonishment, Lord Sunderlin rode up, and Lady S., who endeavoured to dissuade *me* from going as a thing too dangerous, joined the walking party. Wordsworth, with his wife, sister, and eldest boy, came over on purpose. James Boswell arrived that morning at the Sunderlins. Edith, the Senhora [Mary Barker, a friend and neighbour], Edith May and Herbert were my convoy, with our three maid-servants, some of our neighbours, some adventurous Lakers, and Messrs. Rag, Tag and Bobtail made up the rest of the assembly.

We roasted beef and boiled plum-puddings there; sang "God save the King" round the most furious body of flaming tar-barrels that I ever saw; drank a huge wooden bowl of punch; fired cannon at every health with three times three, and rolled large blazing balls of tow and turpentine down the steep side of the mountain. The effect was grand beyond imagination. We formed a huge circle round the most intense light, and behind us was an immeasurable arch of the most intense darkness, for our bonfire fairly cut out the moon.

The only mishap which occurred will make a famous anecdote in the life of a great poet, if James Boswell, after the example of his father, keepeth a diary of the sayings of remarkable men. When we were craving for the punch, a cry went forth that the kettle had been knocked over, with all the boiling water! Colonel Barker, as Boswell named the Senhora, from her having had command on this occasion, immediately instituted a strict inquiry to discover the culprit, from a suspicion that it had been done in mischief, water, as you know, being a commodity not easily replaced on the summit of Skiddaw. The persons about the fire declared it was one of the gentlemen - they did not know his name, but he had a red cloak on; they pointed him out in the circle. The red cloak (a maroon one of Edith's) identified him; Wordsworth had got hold of it and was equipped like a Spanish Don - by no means the worst figure in the company. He had committed the fatal *faux pas* and thought to slink off undiscovered. But as soon as, in my inquiries concerning the punch, I learnt his guilt from the Senhora, I went round to all our party, and communicated the discovery, and getting them about him, I punished him by singing a parody, which they all joined in: "'Twas *you* that kicked the kettle down! 'Twas you, Sir, you!"

The consequences were, that we took all the cold water upon the summit to supply our loss. Our myrmidons and Messrs. Rag and Co. had, therefore, none for their grog; they necessarily drank the rum pure; and you, who are physician to the Middlesex Hospital, are doubtless acquainted with the manner in which alcohol acts upon the nervous system. All our torches were lit at once by this mad company, and our way down the hill was marked by a track of fire, from flambeaux dropping the pitch, tarred ropes, etc. One fellow was so drunk that his companions placed him upon a horse, with his face to the tail, to bring him down, themselves being just sober enough to guide and hold him on. Down, however, we all got safely by midnight; and nobody, from the old Lord of seventy-seven to my son Herbert, is the worse for the toil of the day, though we were eight hours from the time we set out till we reached home.

Charles Cuthbert Southey: *The Life and Correspondence of Robert Southey*, 1850.

Natural Sovereignty

As a boy, Wordsworth could see "distant Skiddaw's lofty height" from his home in Cockermouth. Later, he waxed lyrical over the mountain.

Pelion and Ossa flourish side by side,
Together in immortal books enrolled;
His ancient dower Olympus hath not sold;
And that inspiring Hill, which did divide
Into two ample horns his forehead wide,
Shines with poetic radiance as of old;
While not an English Mountain we behold

By the celestial Muses glorified.
Yet round our sea-girt shore they rise in crowds;
What was the great Parnassus' self to Thee,
Mount Skiddaw? In his natural sovereignty
Our British Hill is nobler far; lie shrouds
His double front among Atlantic clouds,
And pours forth streams more sweet than Castaly.

William Wordsworth: *Poetical Works, 1850.*

A Fiery Warning

Skiddaw's geographical position and ease of access have signalled it out as a site for beacons and bonfires.

Till Belvoir's lordly lerraces the sign to Lincoln sent,
And Lincoln sped the message on o'er the wide vale of Trent;
Till Skiddaw saw the fire that burned on Gaunt's embattled pile,
And the red glare on Skiddaw roused the burghers of Carlisle.

Lord Macaulay : *The Armada.*

Celebratory Bonfire

The 1897 bonfire on Skiddaw in honour of Queen Victoria's Diamond Jubilee was organised by Canon H.D. Rawnsley, vicar of Crosthwaite Church. The occasion prompted one of his inevitable sonnets.

Now let the stars from heaven to earth be shed;
Let beacon-fires with tongues of angel might
Speak clear from plain to plain, from height to height,
Till the whole land with joy be overspread,
Till, girt with gems of flame and diamonded,
Great Britain like a bride in robes of light
Shine forth and say was never such a night
For royal worth and loyalty to be wed,
And when her people on the twilit green
On the dusky mountains, with accord
Shout for Victoria, and around the fire
Sing with one heart and voice, "God save the Queen,"
Let patriot flame from off Thine altar, Lord,
Touch all dumb lips, all hearts with love inspire.

H.D.Rawnsley: *A Rambler's Note-book at the English Lakes*, 1902.

Thunderstorm

The 1902 bonfire to celebrate the coronation of King Edward VII was marred by bad weather: the wind was so strong that barrels of paraffin and tar were blown from the summit of Skiddaw and careered down Millbeck Gill. Skiddaw is renowned for its sudden storms, as a visitor in 1866, echoing Hutchinson's experiences a century previously, remembered.

I have been many times on Skiddaw's highest point, but only once during a thunder-storm, and whatever danger may have attended it, I do not regret having witnessed the sight, which is almost impossible, even in the simplest manner, to convey to the mind the faintest idea of the

134

battling of the elements during a storm which lasted nearly an hour.

When we left the Royal Oak, the sun shone out in all its glory; shortly before eleven, however, the heat was intense, and while the sky was yet perfectly clear, a few low peals of thunder were heard. We were then on the highest peak, known by the dalesmen as the "Third Man", for each peak, as you ascend, is called a "Man" - first the "Low Man", then the "Second Man", and the third and highest the "Third Man". From this peak we stood admiring the vale below.

In about a quarter of an hour, the clouds gathered on the edge of the horizon and in a short time volleys of thunder leaped after each other in rapid succession, and with a louder report, followed by flashes of lightning and very large drops of rain; then the thunder was heard growling in the distance and gradually approximating; the huge clouds of sable hue and confused state of the atmosphere gave sure indication of an overcharge of electricity ready to explode. At length the storm burst out in awful fury, every mountain raised a voice, and the scene was appalling; flash after flash of sheet and forked lightning, and peal after peal of loud thunder, near at hand, followed each other in rapid succession, as if the elements had combined to give a manifestation of their majestic power. The rain poured down in torrents. When the storm was at its height, the wind, which suddenly rose to a complete hurricane, was accompanied by a shower of ice, which, from the great weight and sharp edges of each piece, made it a formidable enemy to stand against, and, to protect ourselves, we lay down and covered the face until the ice-storm had passed away, yet, notwithstanding, the face and hands were bleeding in several places.

The clouds now seemed to sink and thicken towards the foot of the mountain, while the top of Skiddaw became partially clear, with a crisp air. We seemed pending between heaven and earth, as the artillery of the living thunder rattled from crag to crag below. The forked lightning seemed to carve its way through the leaden clouds, and the scene was indeed awful and beyond description.

G.K.Matthew: *The English Lakes, Peaks and Passes*, 1866.

135

Chapter 11: EYES OF THE MOUNTAIN

Loughrigg Tarn

I must not omit to mention, as a kindred feature of this country, those bodies of still water called Tarns . . . The mountain tarns can only be recommended to the notice of the inquisitive traveller who has time to spare. They are difficult of access and naked: yet some of them are, in their permanent forms, very grand; and there are accidents of things which would make the meanest of them interesting.

William Wordsworth: *Guide to the Lakes*, 1835.

Pleasing to the Eye

An early nineteenth century guide reminds us that tarns are a feature of the high fells.

There are numerous other receptacles of still water, which, being too small to merit the appellation of lakes, are called TARNS. When placed in a principal valley (which, however, is not often the case), they contribute little to its importance; and being in such situations often environed with swampy ground, seem to represent the feeble remnants of a once more considerable lake. But in a circular recess on the side of a vale, or on a mountain, as they are generally placed, their margins being well defined, they become more interesting. Reposing frequently at the feet of lofty precipices. and sometimes appearing as if embanked by a collection of materials excavated from the basin which they occupy, they afford ample room for conjecture as to the mode of their formation. Being sheltered from the winds, their surface often exhibits the finest reflection of the rocks and surrounding scenery, highly pleasing to the eye of such as view them with regard to the picturesque; but it is more agreeable to the wishes of the angler to see their surface ruffled by the breeze.

Jonathan Otley: *Concise Description of the English Lakes and Adjacent Mountains*, 1827.

Solitary and Solemn

Tarns may be harnessed as reservoirs: they can also inspire feelings of awe.

The Tarns form another peculiar feature of this country-Sometimes found in the vales, but more numerous among the mountains, they answer the useful purpose of reservoirs, arresting the torrents which would otherwise be precipitated in destructive floods upon the valleys beneath, and affording a constant supply of moisture against the overpowering heat of summer. Lying as they do in the solitary recesses of lofty mountains, at the foot of steep precipices, huge fragments of rock strewed on their shores and heath-clad promontories dividing their black sullen waters, they excite in the mind feelings of melancholy and awful solemnity.

William Ford: *A Description of Scenery in the Lake District*, 1840.

Tarn Bagging

There are undiscovered delights in searching for tarns.

A tarn hunt is by no means unexciting sport; for though all of the more important are named in the guide-books and figured on the maps, still there are a few neither spoken of nor marked, the finding of which is a true discovery to the ordinary traveller, leading him into the heart of many a secret of nature, and showing the form of many of her workings. We get to the back of the mountains, so to speak, on such expeditions as these; and when not to the back, then to the inner depths, where we can follow the track of the forces by which these great things have been done, tracing where the fire has fused and the water wasted; and seeing how the mighty shaping hand has fashioned the mountain world to perfect nobleness, and where it has left rough, unfinished bits, like waste-plots in the great garden: rough bits, where only ferns and moss and heather are flung by the summer's charity and where useless water gathers into useless hollows, idle for the world's work, if glorious for the world's beauty.

Yet not wholly useless; for they all send out small subscriptions to the general fund and at least help to swell, if they do not originate, the wealth of rivers and the bounty of the sea; in which manner they are working members, if unnoted, in the great republic of natural forces. Not that every mountain stream springs from a tarn, but almost every tarn sends out a stream. Then, tarn-hunting teaches the relative position of places almost as exactly as do the mountain-tops, leading by "backs", and "shoulders", and "slacks" and "feet" and over the lower heights straight to half a dozen seemingly irreconcilable districts, each one of which is a day's journey from the other by the beaten track. Thus Easedale and Sty Head in one day must needs include some glorious cross-country experiences.

E. Lynn Linton: *The Lake Country,* 1864.

Rocks and Reflections

William Wordsworth echoed his sister's appreciation of Loughrigg tarn.

Of this class of miniature lakes, Loughrigg Tarn near Grasmere is the most beautiful example. It has a margin of green firm meadows, of rocks and rocky woods, a few reeds here, a little company of water-lilies there, with beds of gravel or stone beyond; a tiny stream issuing neither briskly nor sluggishly out of it; but its feeding rills, from the shortness of their course, so small as to be scarcely visible. Five or six cottages are reflected in its peaceful bosom; rocky and barren steeps rise up above the hanging enclosures; and the solemn pikes of Langdale overlook, from a distance, the low cultivated ridge of land that forms the northern boundary of this small, quiet, and fertile domain.

William Wordsworth: *A Guide through the District of the Lakes,* 1835.

Home for a Hermit

Not surpringly, Loughrigg Tarn has inspired romantic responses. This is the solitude that reason loves!

Even he who yearns for human sympathies,
And hears a music in the breath of man,
Dearer than voice of mountain or of flood,
Might live a hermit here, and mark the sun
Rising or setting 'mid the beateous calm,

139

Devoutly blending in his happy soul
Thoughts of earth and heaven! - Yon mountain-side,
Rejoicing in its clustering cottages,
Appeal's to me a paradise preserved
From guilt by Nature's hand, and every wreath
Of smoke, that from these hamlets mounts to heaven,
In its straight silence holy as a spire
Reared o'er the house of God.
Thy sanctity
Time yet hath reverenced, and I deeply feel
That innocence her shrine shall here preserve
For ever. - The wild vale that lies beyond,
Circled by mountains trod but by the feet
Of venturous shepherd, from all visitants,
Save the free tempests and the fowls of heaven,
Guards thee; - and wooded knolls fantastical
Seclude thy image from the gentler dale.
That by the Brathay's often-varied voice
Cheered as it winds along, in beauty fades
'Mid the green banks of joyful Windermere!

John Wilson: *The Poems*, 1865.

Perfectly Alone

Easedale Tarn near Grasmere is a popular destination for fell walkers. A century and a half ago, it was not so well known.

At the farm house where the car stops, the people will show the stranger the way he must go - past the plantation and up the hill side, where he will find the track that will guide him up to the waterfall - the foaming cataract which is seen all over the valley, and is called Sour Milk Ghyll Force. The water and the track together will show him the way to the tarn, which is the source of the stream. Up and on he goes, over rock

140

and through wet moss, with long stretches of dry turf and purple heather; and at last, when he is heated and breathless, the dark cool recess opens in which lies Easedale Tarn. Perhaps there is an angler standing beside the great boulder on the brink. Perhaps there is a shepherd lying among the ferns. But more probably the stranger finds himself perfectly alone.

There is perhaps nothing in natural scenery which conveys such an impression of stillness as tarns which lie under precipices: and here the rocks sweep down to the brink almost round the entire margin. For hours together, the deep shadows move only like the gnomon of the sundial; and, when movement occurs, it is not such as disturbs the sense of repose; - the dimple made by a restless fish or fly, or the gentle flow of water in or out; or the wild drake and his brood, paddling so quietly as not to break up the mirror, or the reflection of some touch of sunlight, or passing shadow. If there is commotion from gusts or eddies of wind, the effect is even more remarkable. Little white clouds are driven against the rocks - the spray is spilled in unexpected places; now the precipices are wholly veiled, and there is nothing but the ruffled water to be seen; and again, in an instant, the rocks are disclosed so fearfully that they seem to be crowding together to crush the invader. If this seems to the inexperienced like extravagance, let him go alone to Easedale Tarn, or Angle Tarn on Bowfell, on a gusty day and see what he will find.

Harriet Martineau: *A Complete Guide to the English Lakes*, 1855.

Ginger Beer and Apples

For many years, visitors to Easedale Tarn were able to buy refreshments from a hut on its shore.

There is a path leading to Easedale Tarn and up which, if the tourist has any legs worthy of the name, he should by all means climb. His carriage has been left a mile behind at a farm-house, and he must needs dismiss with it all commonplace matters from his mind at once.

141

He is about to be alone with the Genius of Solitude in one of the most sublime of her retreats. When I last visited the spot, I regret to say that Solitude had a companion up at the tarn, who was not a Genius, and who sold ginger-beer and inferior apples.

This is one of the necessary curses of Tourism, that the most exquisite and glorious scenes - and yet whose attractions, of course, materially depend upon their freedom from vulgar associations - are made the emporiums of refreshment for visitors. Killarney and Snowdon have long been desecrated by such practices; but, till lately, our Lakeland was quite free from them. The good man at Easedale Tarn had, of course, a perfect right to turn an honest penny by building himself a hut, where no other dwelling, save that of the buzzard and the hill-fox, had never been, and by putting a boat upon that solemn expanse of dark water where naught but the wing of a bird had lighted before; but could not he instead have locked the gate of the path a mile away and there demanded a shilling of every visitor, or, indeed, done any mortal thing to Easedale Tarn but the thing he has done? We trust the spirit of the great poet who delighted in this spot knows nothing of the sacrilege! Even then, however, the black crags to the west were not robbed of their peculiar grandeur; nor, if we ascended some thirty feet of the hill behind that accursed hut, was Helvellyn's majesty detracted from a hair's breadth, nor the distant valley deprived of one quiet charm.

James Payn: *A Hand-Book to the English Lakes*, 1859.

Sombre Scenery

Tarns can be forbidding and lonely places.

Grisedale Tarn, a gloomy sheet of water, which, to a solitary pedestrian, conveys, with its sombre scenery around, an idea of desolation that on a cloudy day is enough to make him long for the cheerful contiguity of shops, and far from unwilling to exchange a view almost painfully lonesome, for the unromantic locality of Cheapside, with its din of rattling vehicles and its ceaseless stream of eager passengers.

E.L. Blanchard: Adams's *Pocket Descriptive Guide to the Lake District*, 1852.

A Solitary Retreat

Lonely Grisedale Tarn is the ideal location for a hermitage.

Were I a man upon whose life
An awful, untold sin did weigh,
And Heaven vouchsafed not pain or strife
Enough to do that guilt away,
And it were well in mine old age
To build myself an hermitage

I would not choose a savage place
Where, all the heavenly seasons round,
I should read anger in the face
Of nature's bleak and joyless ground;
And winds and streams have voices rude,
Wherewith to mar the solitude.

In yon pale hollow would I dwell,
Where waveless Grisedale meekly lies,
And the three clefts of grassy fell
Let in the blueness of the skies;
And lowland sounds come travelling up
To echo in that mountain cup.

The morning light on mottled stones,
The unfledged raven's clamorous mirth,

The broken gush and hollow moans
Of waters struggling in the earth,
And the white lines of the bleating sheep
Crossing, far up, the dewy steep.

Where from the tarn the shallow brook
By rough Helvellyn shapes its way.
The window of my cell should look
Eastward upon the birth of day;
Nor should the place disfigured be
By garden plot or favourite tree.

F.W. Faber: *The Cherwell Water-Lily and other Poems*, 1840.

Romantic Tales

Several Lakeland tarns have a story linked with them. Tarn Hows, perhaps the best-known of all the tarns, is the scene of a romantic tragedy.

Some few hundred years ago, the inhabitants of these dales were startled from their propriety by a report that one of the Troutbeck giants had built himself a hut and taken up his abode in the lonely dell of the Tarns above Yewdale Head. The excitement consequent upon the settlement of one of that gigantic race in this vicinity soon died away and the object of it, who stood somewhere about nine feet six out of his clogs, became known to the neighbours as a capital labourer, ready for any such work as was required in the rude and limited agricultural operations of the period. He answered to the cognomen of "Girt Will o' t' Tarns" and once or twice did good service as a billman under the Knight of Coniston in repelling roving bands of Scots or Irish who were wont to invade the wealthy plains of Low Furness.

The particular Knight of Coniston, who was chief of the Fleming family, had a daughter, Eva le Fleming, famed for her beauty and

Rydal Waterr

gentleness, her high-bred dignity and her humble virtues. She had a maid, Barbara, who was also deemed beautiful and often as she rode to visit her parents at Skelwith, she drew admiring looks for the elegance of her figure, the ease of her deportment and the all-surpassing loveliness of her features. The only young man to whom she showed the slightest courtesy was Dick Hawksley, the Knight's falconer.

One evening, the Lady Eva and Barbara were walking through the woods when suddenly Great Will of the Tarns sprang out of the trees, seized tbe screaming Barbara and vanished amongst the hazel thickets.

The Lady Eva rushed home and immediately Dick Hawksley and a few more dashed off in pursuit of Will and Barbara. They caught up with the giant and his victim near Cauldron Dub and Will, realising it was hopeless to carry his prize any further, flung her into the flooded

145

beck. Dick plunged in and caught Barbara: the strong current swept them away and the gallant Hawksley and the Lady Eva's beateous favourite were seen no more, till their bodies were found days after on the shore far down the lake.

The pursuit of Will continued with renewed energy and he was finally caught, and amid a storm of vengeful yells and bitter execrations, he was savagely slaughtered. His grave, it is said, may still be found near the beck, haunted by his ghost.

Wilson Armistead: *Tales and Legends of the English Lakes*, 1891.

The Drowned Village

Urswick Tarn near Ulverston has a very different story to tell.

Oh! Urswick's Lake is bright and blue,
And Urswick's Lake is fair:
And 'tis sweet to see how dazzlingly
Each star is mirrored there.

And 'tis glorious, when the full, round moon,
Has climbed the heaven high,
To gaze into that Lake's far depths,
As into another sky.

Down in a lonely, verdant vale,
Where rustic charms abound,
Its waters sleep all peacefully,
With hills encompassed round.

But the peasants tell, that, years ago,
In the time of the vengeful Dane,
A village stood where the watery flood
Now covers o'er the plain.

146

When the sun went down, its red light fell
On lowly roof and byre;
And the solemn knell of the vesper bell
Pealed from the village spire.

When the morning came, the bright sun looked
On a lake's discoloured wave;
For the earthquake's might in the dark midnight
Had sunk that village so fair to sight
In a deep and watery grave.

No time for confession – none for shrift –
No moment the beads to tell;
The child slept sound on its mother's breast,
When that dreadful fate befell.

No warning voice – no wailing cry –
No bell was heard to toll;
But they perished without a priest to say
"God's blessing on each soul".

On St John's Eve there's a wondrous light
Shines brightly o'er the lake;
And men may see a glorious sight
If a boat they deftly take;

For lowly roof and tapering spire,
Their magic form display –
But at morn's first beam, like a pleasant dream,
They quickly melt away.

J. Richardson: Furness Past and Present, 1870.

Local Pride

Urswick Tarn v. The Lake of Como.

It is ever gratifying to find love of one's own country deeply implanted in the breast of any individual, and the powerful hold which early impressions make upon the mind of the true patriot, irresistibly clinging to his heart-strings in whatever clime his fortunes may lead him. Such men are made of the true metal that bears a higher stamp than mere sounding brass or tinkling cymbal, and it is always pleasing to record their observations and reflections when bearing upon the subject just mentioned.

A native of Furness chanced to be employed for some months in the neighbourhood of the Lake of Como, celebrated for its beauty in romance and song, and on returning to his native district was questioned about the scenes he had witnessed when abroad. Having alluded, among other things, to the Lake of Como, he was asked, "What mak of a spot is it?" - to which he replied, "Why, I've heeard a deal o' fine toke about t'pleass, sartenly; but for my part I set noute be't. It's varra lile bigger nor Ossick Tarn and net hofe as nice!"

R. Piketah: *Furness Fells*, 1870.

A Hidden Gem

Glaramara is home to several small but delightful hidden tarns.

Keep away under Great End; if it be a misty day, walking in and out of the clouds as you walk in and out of passages and fields and woods, till you come to Sparkling Tarn, sometimes called Sprinkling Tarn, set not in a cup but in a mere hollow on the top of High House.

Angle Tarn needed the cloud blackness which suited well with its depth under the high fell shadow; but Sparkling Tarn - lying in its shallow basin at the very brow of High House, looking up into the face of the sky and catching the faintest glint of sunshine that falls - seems

148

born only for the light of heaven to mirror itself within - only for the smiles and the joy of the sunshine: a bright-faced, bright-eyed little Naiad resting on the bosom of the old green bill and playing with the sunbeams as they get entangled in her hair. The rim of the tarn is singularly shallow; it seems scarcely high enough to prevent the water from overflowing High House sides and streaming down at every angle, instead of keeping its appointed channel as feeder in principal to Sty Head Tarn; but if shallow, it is broad, with a great promontory of turf and rock - almost an island - plunging into its very heart and giving food and shelter to the mountain sheep, it is very beautiful and remarkable, lying there on the mountain top with only so narrow a ledge of rock to keep it within bounds and prevent it shedding itself all abroad. The proper course of the issuing stream is down a little rocky bed to Sty Head Tarn but not much of a feeder to the Sty Head fishes, for they - no, the anglers - complain that these suffer considerably in food and flesh by the impoverishment of the Sparkling waters, of which the Sparkling fishes have had the first and fullest benefit . . .

Scarcely a hundred yards from this lovely little water-world, you come upon another tarn - your real discovery of the day; a tarn known only to the shepherds, and not even to the guides, still less to guide-book makers. It is a sort of toy-lake, different to anything seen before; oval, surrounded by small, slaty, basaltic-like crags, part with a little grass growing in among them and part a mere piling up of small stones, as if they were miniature crags built by children: a very fairies' lake on which you will come with as much pleasure as if you had fallen upon a royal child among the shepherds or a white enchanted fawn among the sheep. It is called by the few who know of it, High House Tarn; and, like Sparkling Tarn, sends down its little toy tributary into Sty Head Tarn. As the mists steal or send over it, it is the most lovely and most unreal vision of a lake that can be imagined.

E. Lynn Linton: *The Lake Country*, 1864.

149

Chapter 12: CHASMS AND CATARACTS

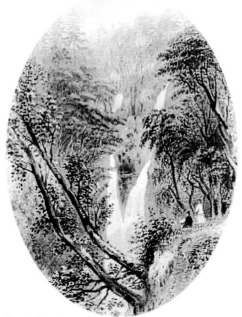

Stockghyll Force, Ambleside, in the grounds of the Salutation Hotek

It comes thundering, and floundering, and thumping, and flumping, and bumping, and jumping, and hissing, and whizzing, and dripping, and skipping, and grumbling, and rumbling, and tumbling, and falling, and brawling, and dashing, and clashing, and splashing, and pouring, and roaring, and whirling, and curling, and leaping, and creeping, and sounding, and bounding, and clattering, and chattering, with a dreadful uproar - and that way the water comes down at Lodore.

Robert Southey: *Letter to Lieutenant Southey,* 18 October 1809.

Artistic Licence

William Gilpin catalogues the guidelines for picturesque viewing of waterfalls.

The *cascade*, which is the next object of our observation, may be divided into the *broken* and the *regular* fall.

The *first* belongs most property to the rock whose projecting fragments, impeding the water, break it into pieces - dash it into foam - and give it all the spirit and agitation which that active element is capable of receiving. Happy is the pencil which can seize the varieties and brilliancy of water under this circumstance.

In the *regular* fall the water meets no obstruction but pours down from the higher ground to the lower in one splendid sheet.

Each kind hath its beauties, but in general the *broken* fall is more adapted to a small body of water and the *regular* to a large one. The small body of water has nothing to recommend it but its variety and bustle, whereas the large body has a dignity of character to maintain. To fritter *it* in pieces would be to destroy in a degree the grandeur of its effect. Were the Niagara thus broken, at least if some considerable parts of it were not left broad and sheety, it might be a grand scene of confusion; but it could not be that vast, that uniform and simple object which is most capable of expressing the idea of greatness.

As there are few *considerable* rivers in the romantic country we are now examining, the most beautiful cascades (which are innumerable) are generally of the *broken* kind. The *regular* falls (of which there are also many) are objects of little value. Though they are sometimes four or five hundred feet in height, yet they appeal only like threads of silver at a distance and like mere spouts at hand, void both of grandeur and variety. And yet, in heavy rains, some of them must be very noble, if we may judge from their channels, which often show great marks of violence - but I was never fortunate enough to see any of them in these moments of wildness.

151

These two kinds of cascades, the *broken* and the *regular*, may be combined. If the weight of water be small, it is true, it will admit only the broken fall; but if it be large, it may with propriety admit a combination of both, and these combinations may be multiplied into each other with endless variety.

The *regular* fall admits also another mode of variety by forming itself into what may be called the *successive* fall, in which the water, instead of making one continued shoot, falls through a succession of different stories. Of this kind are many of the mountain-cascades in this country, which are often beautiful, especially where the stages are deranged and the water seeks its way from one stage to another.

This is the species of cascade which was the great object of imitation in all the antiquated water-works of the last age. Our forefathers admired the *successive* fall, and, agreeably to their awkward mode of imitation, made the water descend a *regular* flight of stone-stairs.

Before we conclude the subject of cascades, it may be observed that, as in other objects of beauty, so in this, proportion must be a regulating principle. I shall not be so precise as to say what is the exact proportion of an elegant cascade. Nor is it necessary. The *eye* will easily see the enormity of *disproportion* where it exists in any degree, and that is enough. Thus, when a mountain-cascade falls four or five hundred feet and is perhaps scarce two yards broad, every eye must see the disproportion, as it will also when the whole breadth of some large river falls only two or three feet. Both would be more beautiful if their falls held a nearer proportion to their quantities of water.

William Gilpin: *Observations relative chiefly to Picturesque Beauty, made in the Year 1772, on several Parts of England, particularly the Mountains and Lakes of Cumberland and Westmorland*, 1786.

A Frightful Chasm

Scale Force at Buttermere has long been on the tourist trail.

An astonishing water-fall that deserves a visit from every tourist whose curiosity leads him to visit these romantic regions. Its fall is nearly 200 feet, excelling that of Niagara about 50 feet. The passage to the basin into which the principal part of the water is precipitated is through a frightful chasm, 100 yards into the mountains, four or five yards wide and fenced on each side by perpendicular walls of rock. Some large trees grow from the fissures near the summit of the mountain and throw a shade on the cavern below, which is of itself sufficiently dreadful without any additional appendages of horror.

When I last visited this cataract, it was in all its grandeur, having been on the preceeding day reinforced by successive showers of heavy rain. The body of water which it precipitated almost filled the chasm, and more violent strife between rock and water was never beheld. The very mountain seemed to shake by the struggle, and the noise, as loud as that of a peal of thunder, was sufficient to alarm the most intrepid ear.

Thomas Sanderson: *A Companion to the Lakes*, 1807.

Surprising Phenomenon

A visitor in 1788 was equally impressed by Scale Force.

Crossing the vale of Buttermere, we entered a most intricate, barren inclosure called Buttermere-scale, which, with the assistance of our experienced guide, we passed with great difficulty. Here, fastening our horses to some rails, we walked about a quarter of a mile to the left to view that surprising phenomenon called Scale-force, and of which no description has yet been given.

At the time we were inspecting this extraordinary chasm, its fall of water was deficient more than half its usual quantity, which gave us a better opportunity of examining every part. It is a wonderful

153

separation of the two rocks, about ten feet wide, and the perpendicular fall of the stream near 150 feet. The rocks are chiefly barren that surround it, but on its margin, as if more peculiarly to adorn this enchanting spot, hang in graceful order both the willow and the ash. Its moist walls are covered by the soft hand of nature with every sweet variety of moss, herb and flower, which form innumerable pictures beyond the reach of art to imitate such excellence.

Stebbing Shaw: *A Tour in 1787 from London to the Western Highlands of Scotland including excursions to the Lakes of Westmorland and Cumberland*, 1788.

Pure Unrivalled Nature

Aira Force on Ullswater has never lacked its admirers.

Airey Force is about a quarter of a mile from the lodge [Lyulph's Tower]. This pretty waterfall is on the small stream that descends from the head of Matterdale and that issues into Ullswater Lake close to the park entrance from Patterdale. A narrow but well kept path leads from the lodge along the banks of the stream to where a rustic wooden bridge is admirably placed for picturesque effect nearly under the fall.

The view is neither grand nor majestical, nor is the splash loud enough to shake the nerves of a lady's lap-dog, but without all that it is an extremely beautiful object, possessing all the rare attributes of pure unrivalled nature pleasingly combined with art. The water descends in two gushing streams from a height of about sixty or seventy feet and forms a complete cross. At different elevations and spanning the torrent stand two rustic wooden bridges, to which several pathways diverging upward from the level of the stream find a way. A more romantic and beautiful spot to ramble away a few hours in, it has seldom been my fortune to witness.

J. Onwhyn: *Pocket Guide to the Lakes*, 1841.

154

Aira Force

Highly Solemn and Picturesque

Thomas Hartwell Home visited Aira Force in 1816 and wrote a description which is typical of early nineteenth century attitudes.

[Aira Force is] a celebrated cataract, produced by the little river Airey dashing over a craggy precipice with a tremendous noise. The way to it is through a winding rocky terrace-road overhung with oaks and other trees that nearly exclude the sun. The fall is audible long before it is approached.

We crossed a rustic wooden bridge thrown over the river to the slippery crags on the opposite side rising in great majesty. The water rushes through a deep fissure, worn by its long continued violence, in two streams - one a little ribbon-like current, the other a foaming torrent - and tumbles down the rock, eighty feet perpendicular height, into a deep basin which has been worn into its present shape by the force of the water impetuously dashing from the precipice through a succession of ages. Above the fissure, as well as on each side of the basin, trees and shrubs form a gloomy arcade and render the scene highly solemn and picturesque. Nearly at the bottom of the fall, the withered trunk of an old oak tree (felled many years since) stands alone and divides the current. The sun, which had been beclouded, now broke suddenly forth and the refraction of its rays among the foaming spray produced a variety of resplendent colours. In its subsequent course through the park, the river forms three or four smaller cascades, which, being picturesquely overhung with trees, would elsewhere be accounted beautiful but here are lost in the grandeur of the cataract, which, by way of eminence, is termed Airey Force.

J. Farington & T.H. Home: *The Lakes of Lancashire,*
Westmorland and Cumberland, 1816.

True Love and Tragedy

Aira Force has its own romantic legend.

It appears that in that very indefinite period popularly known as the olden time a certain knight, who loved a lady and who courted her here in her father's old tower of Greystock, went forth to achieve the hand of his lady-love by performing daring deeds in knight-errantry. His endeavours to please appear to have been crowned with the greatest success, for the lady's heart was gladdened by the tidings that were borne to her from time to time of the gallant knight's prowess. But he was so long in returning and she heard so much of his championship on behalf of other distressed ladies, that a doubt at length stole upon her heart as to whether she was still beloved.

Harassed with these doubts by day, they at length disturbed her mind in sleep and as a somnambulist she would walk in her dreams, directing her footsteps towards the spot where she had been in the habit of meeting her lover. The limit of these dream-wanderings was a holly-tree beside the waterfall where they had plighted their troth and here she would come in her sleep and safely traverse the most dangerous paths.

At length the knight returned to claim her, and, arriving in the night, he went to the ravine to rest under the holly until morning should permit him to appear at the tower and make his formal application for her hand. As he approached the well-known trysting-tree, he saw a white figure gleaming in the moonlight among the foliage. It reached the holly before him; a hand gently gathered a few leaves from the tree and they were thrown with a deep sigh into the rushing stream beneath. He stood amazed, doubting if it were an apparition or a reality that he saw.

At last, convinced that it was his betrothed who stood before him, the knight rushed towards her to rescue her from the danger of the position in which she stood. As his arm was outstretched to save her, she was awakened by the touch and in her terror and confusion she fell from his grasp and was carried by the torrent down the ravine. He dashed in to rescue her and succeeded in bringing the inanimate form to the bank, but there she died in her lover's arms, her latest moments being brightened by the assurance that he whom she loved was true and had come to claim her. In memory of his bereavement, the knight erected a hermitage upon the spot where this fatality occurred and spent the rest of his life in mourning her.

E.L. Blanchard: *Adams's Pocket Descriptive Guide to the Lake Districts*, 1852.

Old Mill on the Stock, Ambleside

An Agreeable Scene

Stock Ghyll, near the centre of Ambleside and easy of access, has always been a magnet for tourists.

As you enter the wood in which the fall is, you hear a sound like the hissing of a tea-kettle. Further on, as the sound grows louder, it is like that of a shower falling on trees. Still higher up, growing yet louder, it resembles the noise made by a drenching storm. At last you come to the waterfall, which is really beautiful. It falls four times, in all about seventy feet. Taking the wood, the gill, overhung as it is with oaks, sycamores, ashes and other trees, and the divided waterfall altogether, hardly can you fancy any scene more agreeable . . . the deep, rocky and rugged bed of the green moss which contrast beautifully with the snow-white foam of the smaller falls, while in the banks are hundreds of miniature caves and hollows interlaced with the roots of trees.

George Mogridge: *Loiterings among the Lakes*, 1849.

Unspoiled Rugged Beauty

A walk to Stock Ghyll is recommended for anyone who wants to put a feather in his mountain-cap.

Many and beautiful are the walks about Ambleside: walks within a reasonable distance for any fair pedestrian and which all but very fine ladies or very delicate ones may take without too much fatigue, and without risk or danger if they are but moderately careful. First, there is Stockghyll Force just at the back of the town, a rough unspoiled bit of rugged beauty, happily for the lake-world scarcely able to be be spoilt even by Improvers, so impracticable is it and so wild.

Over rocks and stones, brawling and leaping in its imprisoned strength, the river rushes on in its mountain vigour - past the bobbin-mill . . . where you may stand on the narrow plank that does duty for a bridge, and, if you have lost any one among the rocks, fancy you hear their groans behind you - past the town and Miller-bridge just below the town, where it makes its last leap before subsiding, spent and dwindled, into the tranquil existence of the Rothay rippling through the meadows to the lake.

Traced up beyond the mill, following the wild path of rock and running water and twisted tree-roots - the rocks below getting larger and more broken, the rift between them deeper and shaiper - the roar of the waters louder and the rush more fierce and rapid - close to where an old oak tree bends over the ravine, with its mossy roots thrust through and through the pathway, while all its weight of stem and branches is flung across the rift - there you come upon the "loosening silver" of the fall with its forked double leap of seventy feet and its thousand little cataracts below.

In the centre and splitting up into four what else would have been one unbroken sheet is the obstructing rock, its bordering of vivid green marking the point to where the waters flow in fullest seasons and its old scarred face grey and naked in the centre. Down below the leap are quiet pools where the water fairies live; and pools not quite so quiet which the passing rush of the torrent disturbs if it does not penetrate; and desolate wastes of pebbles lying dry and many-coloured in the sun; and rocks which the water never wholly covers but is forced to leave midway, falling like a mantle from their shoulders neither crowning nor concealing; and others over which it is just able to lip with an effort and an almost visible strain, as of actual nerve and muscle, each wavelet seeming as if it must fall back before it reaches the edge, but each finally conquering and fretting painfully over; and others with an unchanging crest of foam as the waters dash on triumphantly, burying them body and soul beneath their flow and planting that crest of foam as a mark of their victory - types all three of the will and its several degrees of conquest and tyranny in life.

Through the breaks in the wood may be seen the purple hills and in the crevices of the rocks windflowers and young ferns; and, for those who have stout nerves and know the pattern of the thing they seek, the *pyioia media*, a rare growth of the winter-green found among the rocks in the centre of the fall. But for every one there are sweet spring-flowers in the sheltered corners and glimpses of the purple hills among the green.

On a clouded day, rock and river and hill beyond are all soft and tender and subdued, with no angles or sharp outlines anywhere; but when the sun comes out, the hills look shimmery in the light and the waters are blinding and gem-like; and every pebble in the waste places and every tuft of moss or clinging lichen, every channel worn by the water, and every furrow traced by the rain is seen as distinctly as if it was a picture of mosaic work. Indeed, the whole thing looks like mosaic, meaning by that, startling contrasts of colours and no continuity of sweep or shading, not even in the line of the Fall itself. The Stock, which separates the parishes of Windermere and Grasmere, comes chiefly from the barren heart of Red Screes up by Kirkstone Pass, a desolate birthplace for so beautiful an outcome! Round about both Force and Ghyll is a charming day's ramble, with just enough of difficulty and danger to delight a town-bred tourist and put a fine white feather in his mountain-cap.

E. Lynn Linton: *The Lake Country*, 1864.

Visual and Mental Pleasures

A visitor in 1802 claimed Stock Ghyll Force was probably the most impressive waterfall in Cumberland.

It lies about half a mile to the left of the inn and may be called a double cascade, as the waters rush from two rents in the rock about forty feet distant from each other, and pouring down different perpendicular channels unite into one mighty stream at the depth of one hundred and fifty feet; from whence the blended waters rush with uncontrollable fury over a series of rocky ledges into an unfathomable abyss, the horrors of which are hidden from the eye by some trees that stretch themselves across the gulf. Of all the Cumberland cascades, this, perhaps, is the most impressive, not so much on account of its magnitude as its partial obscuration; not presenting itself to the eye at once but only showing detached parts, it allows the *creative faculty* to be brought into action and thus affords to the mind one of the most pleasurable exercises it is capable of experiencing.

Revd. Richard Warner: *A Tour through the Northern Counties of England and the Border of Scotland*, 1802

Upper Fall at Rydal

Beautiful Theatrical Scene

The falls in the grounds of Rydal Hall, home of the le Flemings, were particularly attractive seen through the summer-house window.

The door was opened and the most beautiful theatrical scene presented itself that can be imagined. The water dashed down a cleft of the finest dark-coloured rock and over the fall was thrown a rude bridge - and, to add to its beauty, a boy with some sheep was passing over at the time. We then ascended the hill to the upper fall above the house, a mighty torrent tumbling headlong from an immense height. About eleven in the morning, when the sun shines on this stupendous fall, it forms a lovely rainbow in the spray. The middle cataract is likewise very grand.

Jane Harriet Schillio: *Journal of a Tour from Bath to the Lakes of Westmorland, Cumberland and Lancashire*, 1836.

Tremulous Agitation

A description of Rydal Falls in 1806 makes full use of the vocabulary of the romantic tourist.

Ascending under a close covert shade about two hundred yards from the mansion house, our progress was suddenly arrested by the broad bed of the Rothay, dashing with a foamy fury over the precipitous sides of a tremendous gill bosomed high in tufted trees. After tumbling with an horrid roar nearly a hundred perpendicular feet, it is hurried down a gradual declivity into a current, perpetually agitated by smaller impediments. Returning hence we dived into a narrow glen, which the spreading firs have veiled in Cimmerian darkness.

After walking some steps, the guide who preceded us flung open the door of a small summer-house in ruins, nodding over the brink of the river. The momentary effect was electrical! and we drew back with involuntary surprise. The suddenness and velocity of these impressions defy every attempt to describe the effect they produce upon the sensations of the spectator. The water of a small basin, hollowed in a bed of stone and darkened by the impending foliage, is thrown into a tremulous agitation by two little streams falling six or eight feet from the clefts of a small shelf of rock. One of them is a broad riband torrent fretting itself into a white foam; the other a little rippling stream whose current disperses as it falls. The fine marble slabs that form the sides of the basin are carpeted by a thick brown moss and the light, which is denied admittance through the trees, is ushered in at the arch of a small wooden bridge above the falls and reflected from the surface of the water.

Benjamin Travers: *A Descriptive Tour to the Lakes of Cumberland and Westmorland in the Autumn of 1804*, 1806.

Sombrous Gill

Wordsworth, who lived for many years at Rydal Mount, was a near neighbour of Rydal Falls. It is not surprising that he celebrated them in verse.

Then Quiet led me up the huddling rill,
Brightening with water-breaks the sombrous gill;
To where, while thick above the branches close,
In dark-brown basin its wild waves repose.
Inverted shrubs and moss of darkest green
Cling from the rocks, with pale wood-weeds between;
Save that, atop, the subtle sunbeams shine,
On withered briars that o'er the crags recline.
Sole light admitted here, a small cascade,
Illumes with sparkling foam the twilight shade.
Beyond, along the vista of the brook,
Where antique roots its bustling path o'erlook,
The eye reposes on a secret bridge
Half grey, half shagged with ivy to its ridge.

William Wordsworth: *Poetical Works,* 1850 .

Grand and Picturesque

Lodore Falls by Derwentwater hold pride of place among Lakeland's cataracts.

At the south end of the lake are the grand and majestic falls of Lowdore, which are considered the finest in the north. In a wet season, when the bed of the river is full, the noise of the falls is said to be audible at a distance of ten or twelve miles. The waters rush down a chasm of 150 feet in depth betwen the rugged sides of Shepherd and Gowdar Crags with prodigious force, and the scene is in the highest degree grand and picturesque. The massive fragments of stone piled up on either side, the

Waterfall at Lowdore

hanging trees which grace their gaping fissures, the rough grey rocks
which tower above all, and the wild stream which leaps, thundering and
foaming, down the rugged precipice, form a picture at once majestically
rude and beautiful.

W.R.Topham: *The Lakes of England*, 1869.

A Singularly Harmonious Assemblage

Only in a season of heavy rain is Lodore at its most dramatic.

The fall of Lowdore presents a singularly harmonious assemblage of the sublime and beautiful. We seated ourselves within the verge of a spacious and symmetrical amphitheatre, from the hollows of which the wild wood hung in picturesque confusion.

The character of this famous fall (the Niagara of England) varies with the season, as might be expected from the nature of its resources. The cataract, which during the floods rolls with uninterrupted volume and impetuous velocity and shakes the mountains with its rebound, dwindles in the drought of summer into a thousand little rills, babbling in the hollows moulded by their continued eddy or fretting to find a passage between the spiculi [sharp points] that start from the rugged bosom of the rock. These at length join and, as if impatient of delay, wind off into a smooth rivulet on its journey to the lake. The variegated tints of the foliage and the rainbow lustre of the tremulous spray glistening in the sun-beams contributed to the splendour of the scene.

We proceeded (the sound of the torrent still vibrating in our ears) through the villages of High and Low Lowdore. A grey-haired man, bent with age and its infirmities, feebly opened a gate and implored our charity. We were surprised to learn that this *poor* man, who appeared to annex a bare subsistence to his employment, was the unenvied possessor of as many acres as would secure to a contented mind the blessings of independence.

Benjamin Travers: *A Descriptive Tour to the Lakes*, 1806.

Fairy Kirk and Fairy Kettles

Caldbeck, best known for its associations with John Peel, has other attractions.

One object of curiosity, however, a few miles from Keswick, may please some particular tastes. It is a water-fall formed by the river, hemmed in by stupendous rocks, situated at the west end of the town of Caldbeck. The name given to this immense gulf is the Howk.

In the latter end of July 1780 I paid a visit to this place and was kindly conducted by Mr B---- Ad----n. We passed over a field behind his house that lead to it and entered a cavern, which is called the Fairy-kirk, that bears some appearance of an artificial excavation, to which the turbulence of the water by frequent deluges has given its present smooth surface. It is said formerly to have been inhabited by Daemons, not aerial spirits but earthly plunderers who, in the feudal times, infested this neighbourhood. After climbing a range of natural stairs, an opening in the rocks at the extremity presented to our view a great fall of water, which, tumbling perpendicularly into a pool, produces a most solemn roar.

Leaving the Fairy-kirk, we climbed over a precipice and approached a bridge above the fall, entirely formed by Nature, underneath which the raging waters have formerly burst a passage in the rock and by frequent inundations have made the present chasms through which, perhaps, the stream has rushed for centuries. In the gulf beneath are several hollows in the earth, resembling cauldrons, called the Fairy-kettles, where, as the traditional tales inform us, the tiny folk performed their enchantments;. . . The rocks that surround this romantic dell are covered on the summit with trees and shrubs, which overshadow the objects beneath and give them a most solemn gloom.

Universal Magazine, 1781

Cauldron, Crags and Cascades

Nunnery near Kirkoswald boasts the Croglin Falls, not well-known but spectacular.

It may, we think, be safely asserted that the Croglin in this last part of its course for nearly a mile, during which it pours along a deep ravine, has no equal. It first enters this savage dell by a fall of forty feet, forcing its way through a cleft into a deep cauldron scooped out of the rock, in which the water is agitated and whirled around in boiling eddies till it finds an escape by a narrow opening in one corner, whence it rushes down several leaps, foaming over the large masses that hinder its impetuous progress. The rocks are piled on each other up to the height of one or two hundred feet, projecting their bold fronts forward over the river, here scorched with lightning, there with ivy green, or grey with aged lichens and mosses.

On the south side, the path is carried round the protruding masses of rock on rudely-framed galleries supported by rough timbers, thus affording the best and most striking views, because the rocks and woods on the northern side, which are the grandest, are seen to the best advantage. At one time you are on the margin of the water beneath overhanging crags, the brook before you rushing furiously over moss-covered fragments and stones, forming cascades of exceeding beauty, whilst the trees waving in the breeze reveal the shaggy rock that supplies their roots with scanty nourishment.

At another, you are on the brink of the precipice, looking down into a dense mass of wood, out of which the twisted branches of the rift oak, stripped of their bark, toss their giant arms amid the skies, contrasting with the deep green behind, while the water is betrayed by its sparkling sheen and softened roar.

William Ford: *A Description of Scenery in the Lake District*, 1840

Chapter 13: WINDERMERE - WANDER AND WONDER

Windermere from Lowwood Hotel

This great water seems to flow and wave about with the wind or in one motion, but it does not ebb and flow like the sea with the tide ... it seems to be a standing lake encompassed with vast hills that are perfect rocks and barren ground of a vast height.

Celia Fiennes: *My Great Journey to Newcastle,* 1698

Superb Scene of Delight

Many tourists approach Windermere from the south. The view of Winandermere, as the lake was called, from the hill on the fringe of the village has inspired much comment.

As we ascended the hill, my friend (who had before made his tour to the Lakes) informed me that I should have a spendid view of the Lake Winandermere and its surrounding beauty as soon as we gained the summit. I was immediately on the tiptoe of expectation; an unknown anxiety prevailed over me; a new scene was now going to be offered to my view, which my imagination painted in the warmest and most glowing colours of delight. The near approach of pleasure frequently awakens the heart to emotions which would fail to be excited by a more remote and abstracted observance. We pursued our way for some time up the hill among the beauties of the lingy moors, till we arrived at an eminence whence "Heaven, earth and the lake smiled!"

We stopped the carriage to contemplate the magnificent scene at leisure. The sun had just emerged from a cloud, from which his rays shed a flood of light and darted a thousand brilliant tints on the vapours that ascend the horizon, and floated there in light clouds, leaving the bosom of the lake below clear as crystal. All burst on our view at once; on each side of the road were the rich purple heather-coloured mountains; in front, the really grand mountains of the lakes. Such a diversity of colours and tints continually changing on the mountains; the shadows of the clouds flitting up their sides and giving a charming luxuriancy of effect to the scenery; the various and changeable colours of the mountains, the rich mountain brown, the dark heather purple, the deep blue distance, the various greens of the trees and the plantations of mountain firs stretching upwards from the very edge of the lake; blue rocks jutting out and appearing through the trees with a *second* scene, caused by their reflection in the waters of the lake, together with innumerable other beauties,

170

which are vividly painted in my imagination, but which my pen cannot describe, all combining made one grand and superb scene of delight. I spoke not a word, all, all was hushed in my soul. I showed no outward appearances of wonder but I felt one of the most inexpressible, enchanting and sublime sensations that ever warmed my soul.

G.M.A. Maude: *A Tour into Westmorland and to the Moors,*1831.

Delicious Elegance

The islands of Windermere frequently excite appreciative comment.

This prince of the lakes is embosomed in a noble winding valley about twelve miles long, everywhere enclosed with grounds which rise in a very bold and various manner, in some places bursting into mountains, abrupt, wild, and uncultivated; in others, breaking into rocks, craggy, pointed and irregular; here rising into hills, covered with the noblest woods; there waving in glorious slopes of cultivated enclosures, enlivened by woods, villages, seats, and farms, scattered with picturesque confusion.

But what finishes the scene with an elegance too delicious to be imagined is that this noble expanse of water, which may vie with anything in Britain except Lough Lomond, is dotted with no less that ten islands, distinctly comprehended by the eye, from some points of view, all of the most bewitching beauty.

John Feltham: *A Guide to all the Watering and Sea-Bathing Places, with a Description of the Lakes*, 1803

The Most Sublime Scene

A letter from Carlisle dated 9 June 1746 records a typical eighteenth century reaction.

We enquired after *Windermere-lake*; we soon procured a guide, then quitted the high road and rode 12 miles over some of the wildest hills in *Great Britain*. We came upon an high promontory that gave us at once a full view of the bright lake, which, spreading itself under us in the midst of the mountains, presented one of the most glorious appearances that ever struck the eye of a traveller with transport. It measures 11 miles in length and two in breadth, and is surrounded on all sides with rocks, woods and inclosures. In some places the crags appear through the trees hanging over the water; in other places, little valleys are seen opening between the hills, through which small torrents empty themselves into the lake; and in all places the border quite round shows itself delicate and beautiful. In the midst of the lake rise several islands covered with trees which greatly adorn the prospect. We stayed here some time to contemplate this surprising scene and then descended to a small village, but neat, on the verge of the lake, where we procured nets, hired boats and spent the day on this delightful water, either in fishing or rowing about from island to island and place to place, exploring the great variety of beauties which surrounded us on all sides.

There is one island in this lake containing 30 acres, with a house and garden; as it is the largest, so it is the most admired; but we visited another which, though much smaller, is greatly more romantic. It is covered all over with trees and edged all round with rocks; at one end rises a mount to a very considerable height above water, on the top of which is a table and seats, cut out of the rock, agreeably shaded with trees. From this enchanting spot, we command a large part of the lake, which, together with the country that incloses it, yields a prospect surpassing all that ever attracted my observation. *Powis-castle* does not exhibit a view more amazing, nor winds more delicate. The transparent waters of the lake extend themselves many miles before us, round which shade rises above shade, rock above rock, hill above hill, and mountain above mountain, even to the clouds, forming the most stupendous theatre, presenting the most sublime scene that human sight can possibly make room for.

Gentleman's Magazine Vol.18, 1748

A Captivating Panorama

Windermere displays its attractions from all angles.

The characteristics of this lake vary considerably as the tourist approaches either of its extremities. The one to the north, in the vicinity of Low Wood Inn and Ambleside, displays a gorgeous array of mountains which can scarcely be surpassed anywhere in their impressive grandeur, casting their mighty shadows, as the evening declines beyond them, over the broadest part of this splendid sheet of water.

The approach to the southern extremity, terminating with Newby Bridge, exhibits nature in the softer features of a more diffusive and less elevated landscape, under the graceful forms of gentle swells and undulations gliding down to the margin of the lake. Various delightful villas, hanging woods, tracts of highly-cultivated land adorning the banks of these bright waters at occasional intervals along the whole line from the north to the south, add additional charms to the natural beauties of this captivating panorama.

Henry Tudor: *Domestic Memoirs of a Christian Family resident in the County of Cumberland*, 1848

Tranquillity Unmolested

The moral effects of Lakeland scenery?

We were all eagerness to catch the first glance of Windermere, and when the lovely lake first opened on the view, a sweeter picture than it represents cannot be imagined. I will, therefore, only note how forcibly it struck a young lady on her first beholding it: she clasped her hands together, exclaiming, "Oh, heavens, what a beauteous scene! Surely no one can be wicked here?" Indeed, any one would imagine that sweet tranquillity reigned unmolested on its banks.

Jane Harriet Schillio: *Journal of a Tour from Bath to the Lakes of Westmorland, Cumberland and Lancashire*, 1836.

A Prime Viewpoint

The "Station", a building on a rocky eminence near the ferry on Windermere, was popular for its fine views of the lake.

An elegant structure, called *Belle Vue*, which Mr Braithwaite has erected for the entertainment and accommodation of his friends. From hence there is a view that baffles all description and sets at nought the powers of the pencil. The scenery, more especially towards the north, is grand and magnificent; a vast sheet of water, twelve miles in length, appears before us, the sides of which are beautifully adorned with luxuriant foliage, shrubs and the coarser kind of underwood, intermixed with rocks of a greyish hue, whose appearance is finely contrasted with numbers of stately evergreens. Added to this, you behold on another side immense hanging grounds, inclosures of various forms, some of them bounded by woods and others by lofty and stupendous mountains.

James Bourne: *Interesting Views of the Lakes of Cumberland, Westmoriand and Lancashire*, 1796

174

Windermere Ferry

Windows on the Lake

The station had coloured glass windows which allowed visitors to view the scene in all four seasons. Accounts of the colour and purpose of the fifth window differ considerably.

The station, a sort of temple built for the express purpose of commanding a view of the surrounding scenery . . . is approached by a winding path entirely shaded from the sun in the hottest weather, as well as from the wind and rain. The station is open to the public and is well worth visiting. The person who shows it resides at a small lodge at the entrance gate leading to the station, and has generally a trifle given to him by visitors, as he has the place to keep clean. The tower is ascended by a staircase and consists of one large room with five spacious windows, each commanding an extensive view, and the

175

beauty of each is beyond description. The windows are of painted glass, giving an idea of the four different seasons, spring, summer, autumn and winter, which are very well represented. A book is kept in which visitors enter their names and addresses. The name of the late Queen Dowager Adelaide is to be seen in her own hand-writing. The spirited owner has often given public balls in the room, and very many yet make a point of taking tea there in a pic-nic fashion.

James Gibson: Handbook to the Lakes, 1851

Trickery

Not everybody was in favour of the stained-glass windows in the Station.

There is some little difference of opinion as to whether the medium employed fulfils the intended object. There can be no question, however, that the artist or the lover of nature will rest amply satisfied with the lovely landscape and all the real beauties it presents, and will regard the "coloured glass" trickery as suited only to the tastes of those whose souls are dead to the higher influences and who fail to realise the "wasteful and ridiculous excess" which is embodied in this puerile endeavour to add to the charms which Nature has so lavishly bestowed on the "Queen of English Lakes".

G.M.Tweddell: Furness Past and Present: its History and Antiquities, 1870.

Naval Heroes

A small building in the grounds of Storrs Hall, owned in the nineteenth century by John Bolton, was known as "The Temple of the Heroes". The description of the house gives some idea of the type of mansion being built on the shores of Windermere by wealthy industrialists.

We again embarked for the purpose of obtaining a view of the country seat belonging to Colonel Bolton, situated on one of the points of land extending into the lake opposite to Curwen's Island. Before reaching it, we passed a small pier, at the end of which there is a handsome square pavilion, containing on it the names of the four naval heroes of Great Britain, Duncan, Howe, Nelson and St Vincent, in large letters. On turning round the pier, we had a full view of this noble building which, in my opinion, is one of the most elegant and beautiful villas in the whole kingdom.

Here there is no useless show, which ought to be confined to dress; no sacrifice of the object of the structure for the sake of external grandeur; no neglect of any thing which the character of the country requires; and yet every thing about the building at once pronounces the possessor to be a man of rank and taste.

The house is of a light yellow colour that harmonises admirably with the verdure with which it is surrounded. The front towards the lake has a gentle semi-circular projection which contains the door, with two windows on each side. The remaining part of this front is lighted by a large arched window on each side. In the second story, the projection above mentioned supports a balcony enclosed by iron rails of very neat workmanship. A glass cupola rising from the centre of the building appears to give light to the rooms beyond the projection.

On our return from the house we met the colonel's handsome yacht proudly gliding through the water in full sail, with the British ensign and pendant hoisted and with the colonel himself as steersman.

S.H.Spiker: *Travels through England, Wales and Scotland,* 1828.

Birthday Celebrations

In 1825, John Bolton hosted a celebration of Sir Walter Scott's fifty-fourth birthday.

Mr Bolton's seat, to which Canning had invited Scott, is situated a couple of miles lower down on the same Lake, and thither Mr Wilson conducted him next day. A large company had been assembled there in honour of the Minister - it included already Mr Wordsworth and Mr Southey. It has not, I suppose, often happened to a plain English merchant such as Mr Bolton, wholly the architect of his own fortunes, to entertain at one time a party embracing so many illustrious names. He was proud of his guests; they respected him and honoured and loved each other; and it would have been difficult to say which star in the constellation shone with the brightest or softest light.

There was "high discourse" intermingled with as gay flashings of courtly wit as ever Canning displayed; and plentiful allowance on all sides of those airy transient pleasantries in which the fancy of poets, however wise and grave, delights to run riot when they are sure not to be misunderstood. There were beautiful and accomplished women to adorn and enjoy this circle. The weather was as Elysian as the scenery. There were brilliant cavalcades through the woods in the mornings and delicious boatings on the lake by moonlight; and the last day "The Admiral of the lake" (Professor Wilson) presided over one of the most splendid regattas that ever enlivened Windermere.

Perhaps there were not fewer than fifty barges following in the Professor's radiant procession when it paused at the point of Storrs to admit into the place of honour the vessel that carried kind and happy Mr Bolton and his guests. The three bards of the Lakes (Southey, Wordsworth and Wilson) led the cheers that hailed Scott and Canning; and music and sunshine, flags, streamers and gay dresses, the merry hum of voices and the rapid splashing of

innumerable oars made up a dazzling mixture of sensations as the
flotilla wound its way among the richly-foliaged islands and along
bays and promontories peopled with enthusiastic spectators.

J.G. Lockhart: *Memoirs of the Life of Sir Walter Scott*, 1837.

Al Fresco Feast

*On 18 May 1805, a group of friends enjoyed a picnic at the Temple of
the Heroes.*

Descend, fairest Muse, from high Helicon's spring.
For none but the fairest can aid me to sing
A theme so jocund - so replete with delight,
The thought of each day and the dream of each night.
I ask not a metre heroic or great,
The joys of a *Pic Nic* - I wish to relate;
More playful the strain and more lively the lay,
'Twill better describe all the sports of the day.
A *Pic Nic* I sing, of the very first rate,
A modernised party - a new-fangled fete;
Where each guest who's disposed to be jovial and gay.
Brings himself and his dinner - his horse and his hay -
Directed by taste, each prepares his own dish
And presents it as cooked up and dressed to his wish;
No matter what kind of digestible stuff,
The only thing needful is - *always enough.*
If the wine is but rich and the eatables sound.
No complaints can be made - no fault can be found;
The appetite sharpened, each anxiously vies
To rival his neighbour in meats and in pies.
The larder is ransacked - replenished the flasket,
And each brings his ratio in his own basket.
Thus a feast in an instant is placed on the board.

179

With the sweets of the season invitingly stored -
Content the grand rule, while each satisfied guest
Eats the thing that's next to him and calls it the best.
The well-seasoned pun and reply fly around
And nought but hilarity's echoes resound.
Here temperance blesses the heart and the head,
For the wit is best tempered - when temperately fed;
Yet it has one objection - and that is not great.
Its origin French - and all French things I hate.

Anon. A Pic Nic in the Temple of Storrs, May 18, 1805 .

Island Beseiged

During the Civil War, Belle Isle was connected with a curious incident.

This island was once the residence of the Phillipsons, an ancient
Westmorland family. During the Civil War between Charles I and the
Parliament, there were two brothers, both of whom espoused the royal
cause. The elder, to whom the island belonged, was a Colonel, and the
younger a Major in the royal army. The Major was a man of high and
adventurous courage and for some of his desperate exploits had
acquired among the Parliamentarians the name of "Robin the Devil".

It happened after the King's death, when the Royalists were in
despair, that a Colonel Briggs belonging to Cromwell's army, heard
that Major Phillipson was secreted on this island. He set off from
Kendal armed, intending to make the Major a prisoner. The Major was
on the alert and gallantly withstood a siege of eight months until his
brother came to his assistance. The Major would not sit down until the
injury he received was avenged.

He raised a small band of horse and set off to Kendal one Sunday
morning in search of Briggs. When he arrived there, he was informed
that the Colonel was at prayers in the church. He proceeded to the
church with speed and, having posted his men at the entrance, he

180

dashed down the principal aisle on horseback into the midst of the congregation. However, he was defeated, as the Colonel was not there. The congregation were at first too much surprised to seize the Major, who, discovering that his object could not be effected, galloped up the next aisle. As he was making his exit out of the church, his head came violently in contact with the arch of the doorway. His helmet was struck off with the blow, his saddle girth gave way, and he was much stunned. The congregation attempted to seize him but after a violent struggle, with the assistance of his followers, he made his escape to his brother's house at this island. The helmet is still hanging in one of the aisles of Kendal Church.

Philemon Slater: *A Tour over Helvellyn to Scale Force*, 1861

A Heavy and Lamentable Accident

On 19 October 1635, forty-seven passengers on the Windermere ferry were drowned.

For the quality of griefe, none knowes it but hee who hath experimentally and personally felt it That Place, which hath hitherto beene secured from the least perill, you shall now see personated a spectacle of Sorrow, where those, who vowed in a Sacred and Christian manner their vowes to Hymen, the Soveraigne of Nuptialls, are now with Tethis to close in wat'ry Funeralls. The occasion of these sad Obits proceeded from a marriage and a market day, which begot to the Attendants a mournefull night.

Windermere or Winandermere hath ever constantly kept a Boat for Passengers, especially those Inhabitants as remaine or reside in the Barronry of Kendall, as all others who may have occasion to addresse their course by that passage to the market of Haukeside or other places adjoining.

To this Boat, upon a nuptiall but fatall occasion, sundry Passengers, and these all Inhabitants within the Barronry of Kendall,

181

repaired, hoping with a safe and secure gale to arrive where no perill had ever yet approach'd. The Boat they enter'd, securely confident, with 47 in number besides other carriages and horses which (together with the roughness of the water and extremity of weather) occasioned this inevitable danger.

Lanch'd had these scarcely to the medth of the water, being scantly a mile broad, but the Boat, either through the pressure and weighty which surcharg'd her, or some violent and impetuous windes and waves that surpriz'd her, with all her people became drench'd in the depths. No succour, no reliefe afforded, for Gods definite Will had so decreed; So as, not one person of all the number was saved; Amongst which the Bride's Mother and her Brother in this liquid regiment equally perished.

Richard Braithwaite: The Fatall Nuptiall: or Mournemll Marriage, 1636

Fishy Business

Windermere is noted for its fish, particularly the rare char. A singular phenomenon occurs as they and the salmon leave the lake at the confluence of the rivers Brathay and Rothay.

There is here a curious problem for our friends the naturalists to solve - in the breeding season the salmon and the char proceed in company from Windermere to this "meeting of the waters" where they bid each other good-bye. The salmon says, "I will make my bed in the Rothay," the char says, "I will make mine in the Brathay." They part, with friendly greetings, to meet no more until early spring, when they descend the united stream in company to Windermere, the char to remain in the lake, the salmon to pass through it and down to the river - even to the sea. The two rivers are equally pure, both having gravelly and in some places rocky bottoms. Indeed, they are to all outward appearance the same, for, like two beautiful twin sisters, we scarcely know one from the other, and whatever condition is favourable for breeding in one river is common to both; yet the salmon and the char select each its own river, not mixing with each other or changing breeding ground from generation to generation.

John Bolton: Geological Fragments, 1869

Imperial Windermere

In the summer of 1797, James Plumptre, staying at Ambleside, wrote a lyrical appreciation of Windermere.

Oh! 'twere endless to declare
Thy charms, imperial Windermere:
Thy prospects, opening to the view.
At every turn delight renew;
The skimming bark, with feathery sail.
Flying before the freshening gale,
While Music's voice in aether floats.
And Echo still prolongs the notes –
What villas on the banks arise,
T'arrest the far-exploring eyes;
Their varied beauties to rehearse,
Might claim for each a Muse's verse.
Yet let not praise quite keep aloof
From Rayrig's hospitable roof;
And ever be the spot admired,
Where learned Watson lives retired,
Like Cincinnatus, tired of state,
And factions of th'aspiring great;
Withdrawn from party's fierce alarm,
He daily tends his little farm.
And, oh! had I my utmost will,
I'd dwell on yonder woody hill:
That humble mansion pleases best,
Named from the turtle's peaceful nest.

But, soft - the rustling leaflets sigh,
Responsive, as the breeze moves by,
In solemn accents, trembling, say
That Storm and Tempest move this way.
From yonder murky, labouring cloud,
Hark! Thunder's voice rebellows loud:
Heaven's crystal portals open fly,
And lightning blazes through the sky;
Wind sweeps along th'affrighted vale;
And pattering rain, with pelting hail,
Commissioned by great Nature's Lord,
Come to fulfil his might word.
In many a mingling torrent fall,
While deep to deep, loud answering, call.

James Plumptre: *A Night-Piece on the Banks of Windermere*
in Thomas West *A Guide to the Lakes of Cumberland,*
Westmorland and Lancashire, 1802

Matchless Beauties

A year later, in November 1798, Joseph Budworth waxed equally
effusive over the lake.

Stranger! or friend! - or whosoe'er thou art,
If Nature in thy nature bear a part,
Together let us view the scenes around
An azure lake, with matchless beauties crowned.
Far to the North, where rugged mountains rise,
With snow-clad tops, oft buried in the skies –
To nearer hills, rich with autumnal leaf,
Where still some luckless fields are seen in sheaf;
Yet, as the farmers view the drooping wheat,
They hear their sheep in healthful language bleat;
Their fattened kine to other cattle low.

184

With all the grateful tenants of the brow:
Cheered by the sound, inspiring Hope prevails,
And well-earned profit turn Justitia's scales.

Let Man with humble thankfulness behold
The altered leaves their splendid charms unfold;
Whilst the great Orb, in majesty displays
The potent focus of meridian rays;
The God of Nature amplifies the scene,
And valleys smile, with every shade of green.

Let other climes their southern wonders boast.
Their wide-extended lakes, midst varied coast;
The golden richness of the setting Sun,
The mellow purple, when his course is done;
The softened fragrance of the evening air,
That lulls the sad variety of care;
The mighty mountains, lessening to the sight,
Till lost in the deep awfulness of Night:
E'en snows eternal and extensive plains,
All! - all! - that vast magnificence ordains –
Be it yours, adventurous Britons, to admire,
With that enthusiasm the scenes require;
Yet, ere we wish, in search of such to roam,
View them in perfect miniature - AT HOME.

Joseph Budworth: *Windermere, a poem*, 1798

A Thousand Various Charms

Twenty years later, in 1818, John Briggs continued the traditional accolade to Windermere.

The waving wood, the sloping hill,
The winding stream, the purling rill,
The verdant meadow's even smile,
The pebbly beach, the scattered isle,
The dashing oar, the swelling sail,
With pleasing solace never fail
To sooth my care and lull my fear,
Along the banks of Windermere.
When Nature pencilled out the scene –
The humble hill, the valley green:
The bleak inhospitable fells,
With rugged steeps and narrow dells,
Secure in which the smiling farm
Or peasant's cot is snug and warm: –
The forest dark, the coppice trim.
Slow shelving to the water's brim: –
In sweetest green its shores she dressed.
And spread her mirror o'er its breast . . .

When Phoebus gilds the pendant wood,
And paints a landscape in the flood,
A thousand various charms combined,
At every turn enchant the mind.
I range the sweetly wooded shore,
Till sylvan charms can charm no more;
Then seize the oar or check the sail,
Half shrinking from the southern gale.
And now what various prospects rise
To charm my ever wandering eyes!

The fleecy clouds swift o'er me fleet,
Whilst others roll beneath my feet;
Suspended in the centre, I
Seem circled in a globe of sky;
Whilst all around a scene appears.
That nature's gayest livery wears.
The light-trimmed skiff proceeds with ease,
And bids me choose what scenes I please . . .
Now, o'er the lucid dome of heaven,
A full charged cloud is northward driven;
The troubled Lake the tempest fears,
Which now a sterner aspect wears.
With murmuring noise, down teems the shower;
On Graythwaite woods, the big drops pour!
No more the Lake in stillness sleeps;
For now the storm, from Finsthwaite steeps,
Across the bubbling surface sweeps . . .

Now laughing nature re-appears
A brighter hue the verdure wears.
Again we choose, as fancy wills,
The hamlets, mansions, cots and villes.
There Belfield shrinks from public view.
Lost in a grove of verdant hue.
Now Bowness bursts upon the sight:
A lovely village robed in white.
Where heaven and earth appear to meet,
Stands Orrest-Head, a dear retreat.
Upon the margin of the flood,
Stands Rayrigg, circled round with wood.
There's Watson's once select abode:
Great champion of the church and God.
Now northward, mountains towering rise,

187

That with their summits cleave the skies;
At whose huge feet, where art is seen
To clothe the ground in varied green.
Is Ambleside, the great resort
Of folks from city, town and court.
Which their excursions tend to make
The little London of the Lake.
From vale to hill, from hill to grove,
Our wandering fancies ever rove;
A dashing cascade charms our ears;
A sudden squall excites our fears;
Then wafting gales our fears compose
And hush our cares to calm repose.

John Briggs: *Poems on Various Subjects*, 1818

Chapter 14: OLD HABITS

Wray Castle, Windermere

Amongst the peculiar customs of domestic life in this part of the country is that of washing only twice a year.

Priscilla Wakefield: A Family Tour, 1804

189

Old Folks' Christmas

Canon Rawnsley recalls an old custom which Keswick still celebrates every year.

I was thinking of the old folk, men and women sixty years and upward, who were to be assembled today in the Oddfellows' Hall to partake of what is known as the "Old Folks' Christmas Dinner and Tea", with whatever entertainment of reading, recitation, song and speech should make time pass pleasantly between three and seven o'clock . . .

I made my way thither towards 3 o'clock in the afternoon. 'Bus load after 'bus load came rumbling up, bringing out of the countryside the guests from distant hamlet and farm. Not less than 400 invitations had been sent out, no less that 180 old folk had responded. The institution was unique in its way. Thirty years ago, it occurred to the writer of one of the best guide books that exists in the English Lake District, Jenkinson by name, an enthusiastic Yorkshireman, who was domiciled at Keswick, that it would be a very pleasant thing to have a social gathering to which all classes might be invited in Christmas week, and to which all who came should feel that they were there, not as it were by charity, but simply met together to chat with one another and enjoy themselves on equal terms as friends. Jeukinson's idea was warmly taken up by the leading townsmen and from that day to this, the annual "Old Folks' Do" has been looked forward to all through the year and looked back upon with pleasantest memory. Surely it is no small thing that opportunity should be given not only for the neighbourhood to subscribe its small mite to the cause of neighbourliness, but that the young men of the town should all work harmoniously together with the landlords of the various hotels and the principal tradesmen to make arrangements for the proceedings and to wait upon their older guests.

Arrived at the entrance to the Hall, I found the local band making brave music. Passing up the steps by kitchens whose steamy fragrance filled the air, I was ushered into a large room decked with much

Christmas evergreen. Five tables reached from end to end, daintily decorated with ferns and flowers. The Vicar of Crosthwaite, the County Councillor of Keswick, the local lawyer, the local bank managers, and some of the leading hotel keepers were seated in the place of honour as carvers, and after a whistle was sounded by the master of ceremonies, all rose to their feet, grace was said, and the Chairman, begging no one to hurry, impressed upon the company that the oldest and youngest were to take time today, and then the soup was served. The leading tradesmen of the town were told off to various tables again. To the sound of the whistle of the master of ceremonies, they advanced and served their guests. At another whistle, soup was removed and the meats were borne into the room. Beef, turkey, mutton, goose were all there piping hot; potatoes, peas, pudding, turnips and all other vegetables steamed on the tables . . . There was plenty to eat, plenty to drink. For those who cared for it, there was beer, but a large proportion seemed to prefer lemonade. . . There was not much talking. Three o'clock was a late hour for many of the old folks' dinner, and they were hungry, but as hunger passed away the talk grew, and very pleasant it was to see the old folk who had not met for a whole year cracking with one another, and to hear the little bits of family gossip . . .

After the meats came plum pudding. Again the Secretary solemnly approached the Chairman and the Chairman as solemnly assured the company that for those who had few teeth in their heads or had eaten so many plum puddings that they had ceased to care for them, there was an abundance of rice pudding prepared, which was very much at their service. Mince pies seemed to be a kind of necessary second course to this plum pudding and rice. Then the whistle sounded again, and cheese and butter and biscuits were the order of the day. So after about an hour, the tables were cleared and grace was said and the bulk of the old folks left the hall for the carpenters to make their arrangements for the concert singing. They returned in half-an-bour and took their seats again at the tables for the entertainment, which was broken half way by an interval for tea and cake . . .

The proceedings ended with the National Anthem and a verse of "Auld Lang Syne", which filled the room and echoed out into Keswick streets, and then, after many a hand-shaking and "Ye'll be here next year likely," "Ay, ay, I whoape sea," they passed back into the town and back to the omnibuses to the far-off farms and hamlets and the Old Folks' "Do" of 1901 was past and over.

H.D. Rawnsley: *A Rambler's Note-Book at the English Lakes*, 1902

Reynard on the Run

Canon Rawnsley describes the Boxing Day fox-hunt, which is still held in Keswick.

I was not surprised to find on the day after Christmas Day that all the men-bodies who were able and strong on their feet had gathered together in the little Keswick market-place by nine o'clock in the morning, to meet John Crozier's hounds and "gang wid 'era for a laal bit of spoort on Skidder's breast". The hounds came twinkling round the Royal Oak corner and stood about the red-coated running hunstman, listening with apparent pleasure to the magnificent chorus of "D'Ye Ken John Peel" with which their coming had been welcomed, and scarce had the sound of "Auld Lang Syne" died away when the whole market-place seemed to take itself to heels, and the black crowd moved up the Main Street and over Greta Bridge and away through Lime Pots by Vicarage Hill, and so down through the meadows, still grey and white with falling snow, towards Millbeck and the Dodd. As one gazed towards Skiddaw, one noticed already dark figures on the white field of sight or against the sky line. These were the spirits ardent for the chase who had gone away, almost with the stars, to take their signal posts on the higher slopes of Skiddaw, but as for the bulk of the field they moved along, a contented mass with the red coat and the white hounds gleaming in their midst, along through the level valley; and these were the wiser, for, as the old hunstman put it, "Fox knaws

192

a thing or two and it's not gangin' up-bank to-daay, thoo may depend on't."

Half an hour after they had passed, I heard the sound of a horn and the cry of the hounds from afar, and I knew the game was afoot and that the Christmas hunt had begun in earnest.

H.D. Rawnsley: *A Rambler's Note-Book at the English Lakes*, 1902

Christmas on the Farm

Winter in the fells was a time for merriment as well as for hard work.

At no place does Christmas produce more heart-inspiring mirth than amongst the natives of Cumberland and Westmorland . . . Among his native dales, the farmer, who is often a stockman more than anything else, can be seen with his hands enveloped in huge mittens of home manufacture, being gloves without fingers and only the thumb being distinct from the lump; often thrusting them half-way into his trousers' pockets; with a fustian jacket well buttoned up to his chin, jogging along merrily to his daily labour, singing or whistling as he goes, scarcely perceiving the dairymaid with her milk-pail in her hand (and often carried when filled on her head) hurrying to the cow-house, where the smell and warmth of the cows makes her often exclaim that it's a pleasure to gang milking through the snow to git among the cows; while the boy cleaning the byre thinks that his job is not so very nice, while she laughs at him for her gratification.

The tarns and ponds or the river on the top of some weir may be seen covered with boys sliding in their wooden clogs mostly, frequently by moonlight, tripping themselves up often when they roll all in a heap. The roars of laughter resound and they think it fine fun to have a breakin like this upon their sliding.

In the frosty or snowy days, the farmers' men may yet be seen upon the smaller farms, where threshing machines are not obtainable, threshing the corn in couples with a flail, which consists of a hand-staff

193

with leather thongs attached to a heavy stick about four feet long, called the "soople"; and occasionally having a little pull at home-brewed out of a jug hid in a hole of the wall in the corner; while in the farmhouse itself, either churning, washing, baking or making mince pies, the wife and daughters of the household are often to be seen at Christmas time, for the entertainment of themselves or some expected family party. In the long winter evenings, card parties are invited, bowls of punch are not uncommon while roast goose and plum puddings form the Christmas Day repast in many a farmhouse and substantial household. All seem merry; the cares of life are left in abeyance as much as possible, for what is the use of repining at losses and crosses at the end of the year. Let us hope, they say, for a good new year and better luck next time, and so on; while the lads and lasses play off charades. Amateur theatricals, glees, concerts, etc. are got up frequently at village parties and many a night's amusement is improvised for the edification of a great number of the community. Tea parties for the aged, Sunday-school treats and Christmas trees are procured for the children, and prizes often given for excellence in singing, drawing and other accomplishments at this season of the year by the teachers of various day and Sunday schools . . .

Such are some of the amusements which Christmas annually produces. It unites the different members of the family under the paternal roof and cements the good-will of each other towards their neighbours. There is often sadness felt from the absence of some near and dear one, perhaps gone away for ever; but as we cannot always live in the past, our future should be brightened by such gatherings and our minds mellowed and hallowed by bereavements as we think of the yearly festivity and celebrate the anniversary of that birth which gave "Glory to God and peace on earth towards men".

T. Gibson: *Legends and Historical Notes on Places of North Westmorland*, 1887.

An Abusive and Foolish Art

Not all Christmas customs were joyful occasions.

In many places, the lewd and rude rabble meet together at this time with a long piece of wood, and force such passengers as they meet, without any regard to their urgent occasions, to sit astride thereon, and force them to alehouses, and upon resistance they break into houses, force people out of their beds and carry them in the aforesaid manner, either priests or other people, to alehouses, and then they use them and abuse them till they join with them in this folly or purchase their liberty with money. This abusive and foolish art they call "stanging". They hale and pull women out of their beds and carry them in scuttles till they join with them or give them money: this they call "swilling". In several places in this time, 30 or 40 rude and lewd people yoke themselves as oxen and have their plough and go from town to town, having their music before them. They tear and plough up their heaps of manure, called in the north "middens". They tear up flag stones and what comes in their way, except prevented by money, which is their design, and many have sustained bodily harm through and by the aforesaid vanities, and complaining to magistrates got no other answer but that these were Christmas casts and there was no law to take hold of them.

The Westmorland Note-Book, 1889

Married Women Only

Various customs were observed at different times of the year.

The Auld Wives' Hake is another Troutbeck festivity, held commonly on old Christmas Eve at the Mortal Man Inn. As the name implies, it was originally observed by married women only, who met to play at cards, gossip, talk scandal, tell nice little stories of dark complexion, and drink tea with brown cream. But of late years the young people, envying the happiness of the good dames, have intruded themselves into the hake and with dances and such giddy modes of mirth have utterly destroyed the sweet, matronly peace and concord which formerly prevailed.

On Good Friday, it is still usual here to eat *fig-sue*, a mess composed of ale boiled with wheaten bread and figs and sweetened with sugar; but it is no longer, as formerly in Westmorland, considered impious to decline the dish for dinner on this day. Neither do the boys now, as formerly, drag the bones of horses and other animals about to the tune of "Trot herring, trot herring, trot herring away". In spring it is also the custom here to eat herb puddings, which may be a reminiscence of the Easter tansies. Cicily, called also "sweet-bracken", it may be mentioned, is here used as a seasoning for puddings, and also for nibbing upon oaken panels which, when dry, being rubbed again with a cloth, receive a fine polish and agreeable scent.

On Easter Sunday all the villagers attend church, even those who have absented themselves from it or any other place of worship throughout the rest of the year. Then the school children are catechised before the congregation, and each of those who have acquitted themselves satisfactorily is presented with an orange and a purple and yellow stained *pace* or paschal egg. Every child must on this day wear something new - if only a bonnet ribbon or a shoe-string - *or the crows will dirty them*. Serving-men at this season have eggs given to them by their masters, which they take to the public-house and enjoy a carousal of mulled ale.

During the week before Easter, the pace-eggers go the round of the valley collecting eggs and money in recompense for the amusement they impart by their fantastic dresses and doggerel rhymes. The party usually consists of five boys, though men sometimes take part in the performance: two of them wear tall conical caps, trimmed with ribbons, and one of these, who represents Lord Nelson, has a ribbon round his knee and a star on his breast. Another is dressed like a sailor; a fourth represents an old hunchback, with a pig-tail, often real, affixed to his coat lap; and lastly there is the personation of an old woman, bearing on her arm a basket for the eggs . . .

Children and older girls also present to each other pace-eggs stained by boiling with parti-colour calico or ribbons wrapped tightly round them. In the neighbourhood, such eggs are sometimes painted with a figure of Christ, flowers or other appropriate device; and in Lancashire especially, where Roman Catholics are numerous, decorated pace-eggs made of sugary material by the confectioners form at this season an important article of trade.

Scandinavian Society: Troutbeck, 1876

Curing Cattle

It was believed that smoke could get rid of cattle diseases.

Of the superstitious practices which have been connected with Troutbeck, none is more interesting that that of the Needfire, or Willfire as it is here also termed, *willfire* being perhaps a corruption of *wildfire*, which is used wth the same import in some other parts and denotes fire that has sprung fresh from its hidden source, untamed and uncontaminated by subjection to domestic or any ordinary use.

The needfire was last kindled in Troutbeck about a quarter of a century ago during the prevalence of cattle distemper, and was then employed as an antidote to the evil upon all the farms of the valley. On this occasion, after the initial fire had been elicited by the essential process of the friction of dry wood, a fire was kindled first upon the uppermost farm in the valley and from thence the occult virtue of the needfire was transmitted by means of burning peat to the rest of the farms in succession, each farm having a fire to itself, kindled from the nearest neighbouring farm, the separate fires being probably an arrangement to prevent the risk of contagion from mingling the different herds. It was considered essential that the fire should be

197

brought to each farm and not fetched by its occupiers; and, as great virtue was attributed to the smoke of the needfire, potato tops and other damp fuel were freely supplied that the cattle might be well fumigated in passing through. At a needfire raised near Appleby about eighty years ago, it seems to have been considered of importance that the plentiful supply of straw provided for smoking the cattle should be of barley only . . . It used to be the custom in Westmorland and Cumberland generally, previous to lighting the needfire, to carefully extinguish all the fires in the locality, a deputation being sent round to every house to see that not a spark remained.

Scandinavian Society: Troutbeck, 1876

Doing Penance

Some customs could be harsh.

Annie Jackson who, in her younger days for the sin of a frail nature, did penance by walking barefoot through Troutbeck Church in a white sheet, with hair hanging loosely down her back. In after life, she kept a small shop and would sometimes relate her penitential experiences to young women who frequented it, adding in the nasal tone peculiar to her the admonitary clause: "Oh! lassies, ye mun all mind yersels, for t'day when I did penance wor t'wettest at ivver rained fra heaven." It is said that the robe in which this transgression was expiated continued until recent years to hang behind the vestry door, and that on one occasion a stranger, who had come to officiate in place of the absent incumbent, mistook it for a surplice and was about to put it on; but remarking its soiled condition, was told by the amused clerk that the tainted vestment was "Old Annie's penance-sheet" and by no means intended for him.

Scandinavian Society: Troutbeck, 1876

Ceremonial Rivalry

On Twelfth Night in the village of Brough there used to be the tradition of Carrying the Holly Tree.

The ceremony originated as a religious custom symbolic of the star of Bethlehem on the advent of Christ's birth, but during the later years of the celebration of the ceremony I should say it suffered perversion from its original intent.

The ceremony consisted in a number of young men and boys procuring a holly or other tree top; the twig ends of all the branches were lopped off and on the stumps were tied a number of torches dipped in candle fat. These on the twelfth night after Christmas Day were lit up and the illuminated ensign was carried all over the town, preceded by a band of music. As is usual in all towns and villages in country places, there exists a certain amount of jealousy and rivalry amongst the publicans and this ceremony was considered a fitting time to test the feelings of the town as to who amongst them enjoyed the most esteem. Accordingly, each publican offered as much ale or other drink as he could afford to the party that would by sheer force land the blackened emblem on to his premises after the torches had burned themselves out.

Generally the figure was dropped on the bridge, and the last time I recollect seeing it, the contest lay between the Swan Inn and the Black Bull. Old Tommy McGee, the host at the former place and a rather noted character, succeeded in securing the coveted honour by dint of outbidding his opponents in the amount of drink. The ceremony always seemed to end in a few free fights, with blackened faces and any amount of drunkenness. Perhaps there might be a dance at the place where the victory rested but of this I am not certain. The advent of the police system put an end to the ceremony.

The Westmorland Note-Book, 1889

199

Economical with the Truth

At Temple Sawerby there was an unusual custom: its equivalent still takes place annually in West Cumbria.

At a village in Westmorland called Temple Sowerby, perhaps if not the *most*, at least *one* of the most beautiful in the North of England, there has been, "from time whereof the memory of man is not to the contrary", and still is, a custom on the 31st day of May for a number of individuals to assemble on the green and there propose a certain number as candidates for contesting the various prizes then produced, which consist of a grindstone as the first prize; a hone or whetstone for a razor as the second; and whetstones of an inferior description for those who can only reach a state of mediocrity in "the noble art of lying".

The *people* are the judges. Each candidate in rotation commences a *story* such as his fertile genius at the moment prompts; and the more marvelous or improbable his story happens to be, so much the greater chance is there of his success. After being *amused* in this manner for a considerable length of time, and awarding the prizes to the most deserving, the host of candidates, judges, and other attendants adjourn to the inns, where the sports of the day very often end in a few splendid battles.

There is an anecdote very current in the place of a late Bishop of Carlisle passing through in his carriage on this particular day, when, his attention being attracted by the group of persons assembled together, he very naturally inquired the cause. His question was readily answered by a full statement of facts, which brought from his lordship a severe lecture on the iniquity of such a proceeding, and at the conclusion he said, "For my part, I never told a lie in my life". This was immediately reported to the judges, upon which, without any dissent, the hone was awarded to his lordship as most deserving of it, and, as is reported, it was actually thrown into his carriage.

The Westmorland Note-Book, 1889

Fragrant Rushes Strewed

At the rush-bearing service, a special hymn is sung. This is the Ambleside Rush-bearing Hymn, composed by the Revd. Owen Lloyd in 1835.

Our fathers to the House of God,
As yet a building rude,
Bore offerings from the flowery sod,
And fragrant rushes strewed.

May we, their children, ne'er forget
The pious lesson given,
But honour still, together met,
The Lord of Earth and Heaven!

Sing we the good Creator's praise,
Who sends us sun and showers,
To cheer our hearts with fruitful days.
And deck our world with flowers!

These, of the great Redeemer's grace.
Bright emblems here are seen!
He makes to smile the desert place
With flowers and rushes green!

Revd. Owen Lloyd: *Ambleside Rushbearing Hymn*, 1835

Dan Birkett - Jigger Extraordinary

A visitor to Grasmere on 21 July 1827 reveals what happened after the rush-bearing.

The procession over, the party adjourned to the ballroom, a hay-loft, where the country lads and lasses tripped it merrily and heavily.

Billy Dawson, the fiddler, boasted to us of having been the officiating minstrel at this ceremony for the last six-and-forty years.

Amongst the gentleman dancers was one Dan Birkett. He introduced himself to us by seizing my coat-collar and saying, "I'm old Dan Birkett of Wythburn, sixty-six years old, not a better jigger in Westmorland." On my relating this to an old man present, he told me not to judge of Westmorland manners by Dan's, for, said he, "You see, sir, he's a Statesman, and has been to Lunnon, and so takes liberties". In Westmorland, farmers residing on their own estates are called Statesmen.

The dance was kept up till a quarter to twelve, when a livery servant entered and delivered the following verbal message to Billy: "Master's respects and will thank you to lend him the fiddle-stick." Billy took the hint - the Sabbath was now at hand and the Pastor of the Parish had adopted this gentle mode of apprizing the assembled revellers that they ought to cease their revelry. The servant departed with the fiddle-stick, the chandelier was removed and when the village clock struck twelve, not an individual was to be seen out of doors in the village.

William Hone: *Table Book,* 1827

Chapter 15: A MEDLEY OF MAVERICKS

Ennerdale

John Gate of Lorton, ninety-four years old, and his wife, Janet, two years younger, buried their son aged seventy-five. On returning from the funeral, the old man said, "Ay! ay! Janet, it's ower now! Ah tell't thee many a time we wad nivver rear him."

G.D. Abraham: *Motor Ways in Lakeland*, 1913

Royal Family

Patterdale could boast its own King and Queen.

Concerning the origin of the royal family of Patterdale, there are various conjectures; the most probable annals of the house are briefly these. On a sudden emergency, during one of those Scottish irruptions into our northern counties, which so frequently occurred in the earlier periods of our history, a chieftain was wanted to embody and command the shepherds of the dale. In this crisis, an enterprising peasant of the name of Mounsey volunteered his services as the leader of his countrymen: his offer was accepted and such were his vigilance and activity that he succeeded in routing the invading army. He was accordingly crowned amid the acclamations of victory, and was proclaimed King of Patterdale, a title which has hereditarily been possessed by his male descendants to the present time.

J. Farington & T.H. Home: *The Lakes of Lancashire,*
Westmorland and Cumberland, 1816.

Meanest of Monarchs

However true the above explanation is (and other accounts are not so kind), by the end of the eighteenth century the royal house had fallen into disrepute.

[John Mounsey] is now in his 93rd year and had a paternal estate of from £150 to £200 a year, which has always given the (imaginary) title of *King of Patterdale* to its possessor: it is said, from being formerly exonerated from some particular tax, which might be owing to its very *remote* situation and not worth gathering.

By his niggardly parsimoniousness he has realised his fortune, according to some, to £600, by many to £800 a year; and I have even heard him said to be worth £40,000. A strong constitution gave him an opportunity of being laborious and his industry kept pace with *his desire of gain*. He knew to omit getting one shilling was a certain loss of one penny a year for ever, besides compound interest, that accumulating consideration to THE MISERS of the day.

He had many ponies that he kept upon the common land, which he was entitled to from his landed property in the parish. Upon these *lean* beasts, he carried his own charcoal over the mountains to the different forges. He used to throw his hat in their faces to see if they were able to perform the journey: those that did not mind were lucky enough to remain at home and those which ran aside were thought of sufficient strength.

He was reckoned the best boatman between Patterdale and Dunmallart Head, and he used to convey his own slate and wood, or, when other people wanted him, for a trifling sum per load. He was once deeply laden with the latter and was driven by a violent gale of wind upon the largest island. In this situation he remained with his assistant two days. The poor fellow, expecting a short passage, had made no provision. His majesty always carried bread and cheese in his pocket to avoid going to alehouses, although he was never known to refuse when he was *offered to be treated*. When he wanted to eat, he told the man he would go to the other side of the island to see if the wind was likely to change; he then *gormandized* away and made the man believe he had only been to look after the weather.

I must now mention a custom he has long practised which saves him the expense of providing meals at home: to use his own words, he calls them "Entertainments". He lets some fields and small houses, as expressed in the agreement, for so many dinners and suppers, taking care that what are to him dainties are provided for each separate day.

In his tea-drinkings, he takes from ten to fourteen cups, using an immoderate quantity of sugar, of which he is very fond - he generally carries some loose in his pocket . . .

There are numberless stories of him throughout the country in which his cunning was always conspicuous, and only *in his amours* has he been (some-times) over-reached. These are more funny to hear than it would be decent to relate.

Joseph Budworth: *A Fortnight's Ramble to the Lakes*, 1795.

Regal Rags

The Queen of Patterdale owned no royal robes and had an inordinate attachment to the bottle.

We had not proceeded far before we met an old woman with an earthen bottle in one hand and a crooked stick in the other; an old cloth (or what was once a *whole* handkerchief) was bound round her head, with dirty remnants of a gown. On her turning round, I thought of the "Old Hag picking dry sticks and mumbling to herself". I had prepared my penny, when we were struck by a quick voice, "*A fine evening, gentlemen!*" Seeing the people leave their cottages and the hay-makers lean over the gates, we concluded, and not wrongfully, it was the Queen's betattered self.

We followed her to the public-house and were surprised at our reception, though we had heard stories that ought not to have made us so. My friend entered into conversation with her majesty, when I felt myself so emboldened by her gracious familiarity, I drew my chair towards her and called for some gin. I own myself wrong in this, particularly as her majesty said she had not ate any thing for two days, and, although it was a favourite liquor, she would not taste it, but said, "I want some ale to feed my stomach" - which proves it must be very nourishing and that the dregs, as one of our old poets calls them, turn to food . . .

She desired the landlady to fill her bottle to take home with her and then told us the King had broke her hand and knee with his stick. This, we suspected, was only to show us as fair a hand as any queen's whatever, disgraced by a filthy pair of woollen mittens curling half up her arms . . .

She then bridled up and allowed that she had *abundance* of money and that she spent a shilling a day in drink but very little in meat, "and to be sure I was very handsome when young and *not with child* when married. I was a *bold* woman to venture upon so stout a man as the king, but he is now grown an old fool" . . .

The king was observed creeping towards the house. I could not help feeling respect; he had so fine a furrowed face, his head inclined towards the right shoulder, with a ragged handkerchief tied under his chin, and his coat was much torn. He sat upon the table and told her with a feeble voice he was come to take her home. She not only abused him but struck him twice and then gave him a glass out of her bottle to make amends . . .

The queen made so many attacks upon her bottle, she became more noisy and swore she had been drunk for two days, "and as for going to church, I have not been in one this seven years." "Oh, yes, Madam," said the landlady, "you know you was when Mr Myers preached and you smoked your pipe in church". After every replenish she increased in noise . . . We were now at tea and she said and sang such droll things, it burst through my nose and almost choked me. We perceived she was growing worse and as we had seen *quite* sufficient of Patterdale royalty, we paid our bill and made good our retreat.

Joseph Budworth : *A Fortnight's Ramble to the Lakes*, 1795

A Thrifty Parson

Mr Mattinson of Martindale was a very different character from the King of Patterdale.

Mr Mattinson was minister of this place for sixty years and died Jan. 31, 1766. His stipend till within twenty years of his death was only twelve pounds per annum and (though augmented from Queen Anne's Bounty) never exceeded eighteen. On this income he married and brought up four children, and when he died at the age of eighty-three he left a thousand pounds to his family.

With that singular simplicity and inattention for forms which characterize a country like this, he himself read the burial service over his mother; he married his father to a second wife and afterwards buried him. The first infant whom he baptized after he had received holy orders, when she was nineteen years old agreed to marry him and he published their banns of marriage in his church. He himself married his four children, from whom he saw seventeen grandchildren spring before his death.

With so small a stipend as the above, it appears scarcely credible even that a miser should be able to accumulate such a sum, but it should seem that Mattinson had one or two other resources which essentially aided his purse, though even with these additions it is sufficiently extraordinary that he should have left so large an amount behind him.

He and his wife carded and spun that part of the tithe wool which fell to his lot, namely one third; from a school that he taught he added five pounds per annum to his income. His wife was equally expert as a midwife, performing her obstetrical operations for the small sum of *one shilling*! Her profits, however, on these occasions were further increased by some culinary perquisites, as, in compliance with an ancient custom, she invariably officiated as cook at the christening dinner. On the day of her nuptials, her father is said to have boasted that his two daughters were married to the two best men in Patterdale - *the priest and the bagpiper*! The property amassed by the singular economy of Mattinson proved of little benefit to its possessors; after his death it was squandered by his widow and children and she was obliged to seek an asylum in the College of Matrons at Wigton for the widows of indigent protestant clergymen.

J. Farington & T.H. Home: *The Lakes of Lancashire, Westmorland and Cumberland*, 1816.

A Maverick Museum Keeper

Peter Crosthwaite, who owned a museum in Keswick, employed unusual methods of attracting customers. William Gell visited the museum in 1797.

His collection chiefly consists of mineral productions and those Indian bows, caps and ornaments which are to be found in every museum. He had a collection of coins, which I did not examine, the chair of Ld Derwentwater, a Chinese gong which produced a most thundering sound, and an instrument of the staccato kind, made of stone of which he pretends to have found six notes in the proper musical succession. He also sells his own maps of the lakes which have the character of the nicest accuracy in every respect. His daughter seems an elegant woman and more worth seeing than any thing else in his house.

As to himself, he is seated in a gouty chair and drums in one corner of the room, like a fool, to the noise of a barrel organ, while he has mirrors in every direction at the windows, by which he sees every carriage that comes from any of the neighbouring towns, though he sits not near to any of the windows himself. The organ strikes up if any one passes and his horrible drum is thumped, at the same time that the old woman runs upstairs and rattles away at the gong in a manner that cannot fail to attract the notice of the unfortunate strangers in the street.

William Gell: *A Tour in the Lakes* 1797

Fantastic Gew Gaws

William Gell found little to applaud in the eccentric activities of Joseph Pocklington on his island in Derwentwater.

The taste of Mr Pocklington in buildings and decorations is so remarkable that I cannot omit to mention a few of his singularities. On making the foundation for his cellars and house on the island was found a great stone: this, though the architect wished it to remain as an excellent foundation, he resolved to fix it upright before his house and at great expense had it placed there. A druid temple was the next thing to empty his genius and accordingly he collected a number of large stones, placed them in a circle and had them fixed upright on the southern shore. Unfortunately for all lovers of British antiquity, a storm arose in the lake and the waves washed down in one night the labours of some days. On the other side, a venerable white-washed gothic building rears its august head in all the pride of pasteboard antiquity. A church, Faro batteries and four or five canon painted white make up the whole of this miraculous assemblage of beauties and surround the enchanted island. I say enchanted for 'tis plain nature never formed in her most sportive moments such an awkward jumble of fantastic gew gaws.

He has sold this spot to Mr Peachy and means to retire to Barrow Cascade Hall, where, if possible, he has outdone himself in ridiculous fancies. The house is not very particular but a white embattled hermitage is situated on an eminence near it, where he has offered half-a-crown a day to anyone who will live in it, provided the wretch will submit to his conditions, which are these. The hermit is never to leave the place or hold conversations with anyone for seven years, during which time he is neither to wash himself or cleanse himself in any way whatever but is to let his hair and nails both on hands and feet grow as long as nature will permit them. Though the reward is certainly great, yet the happiness of the situation is such that he has never yet been able to persuade any one to accept his proposals. In short, all his white buildings and ornaments contribute to diminish the simple beauty of the lake, which is without exception otherwise the finest piece of water I have yet seen in these parts.

William Gell *A Tour in the Lakes 1797* .

Simple Wisdom

Alexander Pearson records a memorable meeting.

(The writer) happened to be passing through the churchyard as the funeral bell was tolling, and meeting Jane [Craston] said, "Hello, Jane, whose funeral is it today?" She said, "Why, it's nobbut Mrs So and So's." Not having heard of it, he said, "Oh, I didn't know she was dead," which immediately produced the reply, "Well, wat wi' aw these new-fangled trances and sic like trash, I don't know missel for a certainty, but as t'sexton's dug her grave and her funeral's ordered, we must bury on t'speculation as she is."

Alexander Pearson: *Annals of Kirkby Lonsdale and Lunesdale in bygone days*, 1930

Marital Disharmony

When strong tempers meet and marry, life can be far from rosy.

About the year 1825, there lived at Bothel in Cumberland a farmer named Billy Briscoe, who had married a widow, and a wealthy one for that part of the country, since her fortune was £60 a year. But, unfortunately, she had also a strong will and high temper and, as his were of the same character, the match did not prove a happy one. The ill-assorted couple were always quarrelling. If anything went amiss in the house or the farm, the husband at once threw the blame on his wife, who for her part was never at a loss for an angry retort.

Things had gone on for some time in this wretched way, when in despair the husband applied to a wise woman for a charm to protect him from his wife's evil eye. On receipt of a guinea, she gave him two pieces of paper, each about three inches square, closely covered with writing, directing that one piece should be sewn inside his waistcoat and the other fastened within the cupboard door. This was done and the change that ensued was wonderful. All was peace and goodwill.

The cat and the dog were transformed into a pair of turtledoves.

But the harmony was, unhappily, of no long duration. After a few months, the waistcoat was thoughtlessly popped into the washtub and the charm disappeared among the suds, while about the same time its counterpart was swept off the cupboard door during a grand house-cleaning. The spell was broken; peace was over and the house more miserable than ever. The unhappy wife told all this to my informant who, as a last resort, asked her why she did not go back to her own friends, since she could not make her husband happy. "I've thought of that," she replied, "but my money's here and how could I go away and leave other people to eat my meat?"

William Henderson: *Notes on the Folklore of the Northern Counties of England and the Borders*, 1866.

An Unfortunate Misunderstanding

Legal books, in the wrong hands, can lead to unexpected consequences.

A story is told of two worthies, who were taking an active part in a trial, from the neighbourhood of Little Asby, who had a book on law which had been lent to them by a solicitor who had practised in Appleby in former times. The book related to pains and penalties for doing certain things, as well as the law relating to real property. They bad, we presume, been successful in their suit against the other litigants and coming after midnight through the village of Hoff in great glee, they perceived the odour of fried bacon. They thereupon went to the cottage whence the odour came and there found a man engaged in frying bacon. The one who was supposed to be posted up in the law-book said to his companion, "There is a law against frying bacon in that book we had: we will take this fellow before the magistrates at Appleby." The man protested but they, being the stronger party, compelled him to go with them, thinking by this means they could pocket the money due to the informants. The magistrate opened his eyes with astonishment at the charge but they persisted that it was in the book which had been lent to them. He asked for the book, which was pretty well thumbed, and the clause was read thus by him: "Anyone firing a beacon after twelve o'clock at night is liable to the penalty of a fine, or in default, imprisonment, half the fine to go to the informant." Only a slight mistake but a substantial difference between frying bacon and firing a beacon.

Thomas Gibson: *Legends and Historical Notes on Places of North Westmorland*, 1887

Chapter 16: Retrospect

Grasmere from Red Bank

They appeal alike to the eye, the feelings and the fancy; they teem with the varieties of majesty and loveliness. If they astound not with alpine masses clad in eternal snows, with fearful abysses which torture the shrinking vision, nor with great azure lakes, whose banks glitter with palaces, they present charms which affect the mind in a more harmonious and equally perduring manner; if they linger in the imagination less to electrify than to soothe, they achieve the great end of retrospection, which is rather a gentle passage of mild emotions than a series of abrupt and powerful transitions.

M.A. Leigh: *Guide to the Lakes*, 1830

The Lakes for Everyman

By the middle of the nineteenth century, the Lake District was beginning to be a popular tourist destination.

A journey to the Lakes, until very recently, was considered a feat of some consequence and confined to the wealthy few. It is now open to the many and within the command of a large portion of the industrious community who, shuffling off their working coil, can launch into the sweet scenes of nature at convenient intervals and at a trifling expense of time and money. In something less than twelve hours, it is now possible to reach Lancaster from London, and, in four hours more, the banks of Windermere, where, with knapsack on back, a stout stick, a light heart, a moderately-filled purse,and the rest of the travelling etceteras, the tourist can commence an excursion to the Lakes in right good earnest and with the tolerable assurance of enjoying an agreeable and interesting ramble.

J. Onwhyn: Onwhyn's Pocket Guide to the Lakes, 1841

The Stranger at the Lakes

A local poet, Charles Williams of Kentmere, who lived around 1800, left his impressions of the visitors.

> When summer suns lick up the dew
> And all the heavens are painted blue,
> 'Tis then with smiling cheeks we view
> The stranger at the Lakes.

> When morning tips with gold the boughs
> And tinges Skiddaw's cloud-kissed brows,
> Then round the lake the boatman rows
> The stranger at the Lakes.

When grey-robed evening steps serene
Across the sweetly varied green,
Beside some cascade may be seen
The stranger at the Lakes.

Embosomed here, the rustic bard,
Who oft has thought his fortune hard,
Is pleased to share the kind regard
Of strangers at the Lakes.

He whose ideas never stray
Beyond the parson's gig and gray,
Stares at the carriage and relay
Of strangers at the Lakes.

As by his cot the phaeton flies,
The peasant gapes with mouth and eyes
And to his wondering family cries,
"A stranger at the Lakes!"

Sometimes when brewers' clerks appear,
And Boniface is short of gear,
He says, "Kind sirs, we've had this year
Few strangers at the Lakes."

At Christmas, Poll, the barmaid, shows
Her lustre gown and new kid shoes,
And says, "I tipped the cash for those
From strangers at the Lakes."

But could the post-horse neighing say
What he has suffered night and day,
'Tis much, I think, if he would pray
For strangers at the Lakes.

The Westmorland Note-Book, 1889

Paradise Invaded

Not all residents welcomed the tourists - even in the mid-1800s: Harriet Martineau certainly didn't.

Summer brought a succession of visitors - very agreeable, but rather too many for my strength and repose. I began to find what are the liabilities of Lake residents in regard to tourists. There is quite wear and tear enough in receiving those whom one wishes to see; one's invited guests or those introduced by one's invited friends. But these are fewer than the unscrupulous strangers who intrude themselves with compliments, requests for autographs, or without any pretence whatever. Every summer they come and stare in at the windows while we are at dinner, hide behind shrubs or the corner of the house, plant themselves in the yards behind or the field before; are staring up at one's window when one gets up in the morning, gather handfuls of flowers in the garden, stop or follow us in the road, and report us to the newspapers. I soon found that I must pay a serious tax for living in my paradise: I must, like many of my neighbours, go away in "the tourist season". My practice has since been to let my house for the months of July, August and September - or for the two latter at least, and go to the sea or some country place where I could be quiet.

I do not know that a better idea of the the place could be given than by the following paragraphs from a palpable description of our little town (under the name of Haukside - a compound of Hawkshead and Ambleside) which appeared some time since in "Chambers's Journal."

"The constitution of our town suffers six months of the year from fever and the other six from collapse. In the summer-time our inns are filled to bursting; our private houses broken into by parties desperate after lodgings; the prices of every thing are quadrupled; our best meat, our thickest cream, our freshest fish, are reserved for strangers; our letters, delivered three hours after time, have been opened and read by banditti assuming our own title; ladies of quality, loaded with tracts,

217

fusillade us; savage and bearded foreigners harass us with brazen wind instruments; coaches run frantically towards us from every point of the compass; a great steam-monster ploughs our lake and disgorges multitudes upon the pier, the excursion-trains bring thousands of curious vulgar, who mistake us for the authoress next door and compel us to forge her autograph; the donkeys in our streets increase and multiply a hundredfold, tottering under the weight of enormous females visiting our water-falls from morn to eve; our hills are darkened by swarms of tourists; we are ruthlessly eyed by painters and brought into foregrounds and backgrounds as "warm tints" or "bits of repose"; our lawns are picnicked upon by twenty at a time and our trees branded with initial letters; creatures with introductions come to us and can't be got away; we have to lionise poor, stupid and ill-looking people for weeks, without past, present or future recompense; Sunday is a day of rest least of all and strange clergymen preach charity-sermons every week with a perfect kaleidoscope of religious views. The fever lasts from May until October.

When it is over, horses are turned out to grass and inn-servants are disbanded; houses seem all too big for us; the hissing fiend is "laid" upon the lake; the coaches and cars are on their backs in outhouses, with their wheels upwards; the trees get bare, the rain begins to fall, grass grows in the streets, and Haukside collapses.

Our collapse lasts generally from November to May. During this interval, we residents venture to call upon each other. Barouches and chariots we have none but chiefly shandrydans and buggies; we are stately and solemn in our hospitalities and retain fashions amongst us that are far from new; we have evening parties very often, and at every party - whist! Not that it is our sole profession; not that it is our only amusement; it is simply an eternal and unalterable custom - whist! We have no clubs to force it into vigour: the production is indigenous and natural to the place. It is the attainment of all who have reached years of maturity; the dignity of the aged and the ambition of the young; a little whirling in the dance, a little leaning over the piano, a little attachment to the supper-table, a little flirting on both sides - all this is at Haukside as elsewhere; but the end, the bourne to which male and female alike tend at last after experiencing the vanity of all things else, and from which none ever returns, is - the whist-table."

Harriet Martineau: *Autobiography*, 1877.

Pastoral and Becoming

Through other eyes, Ambleside could look rather more appealing.

The little jewel, Ambleside, which is thus so gorgeously set, is itself not without some graces peculiarly its own. What is old about it, is pastoral and becoming. What is new is, upon the whole, well-ordered and not too pretentious. It has a central Market Place, a handsome Mechanics' Institution, a Town Hall; a wonderful bridge-cottage - very uncomfortable, we should imagine, as a private residence, but undeniably picturesque - which has made its appearance in every London water-colour exhibition every summer and has of late become the prey of the photographist; a bobbin mill, which has suffered the like indignities; a church, which has revenged itself in part by its hideous spire for the same attempted insults, but which is a handsome edifice for all that to our mind, both inside and out.

The streets are none of your rectangular monotonous affairs, with squares and crescents, but perform eccentric curves in all directions - darting away sometimes downward under archways but chiefly ascending perpendicular "pitches" which, to see a coach attempting with only four horses, seems like madness, and which to essay ourselves upon that equipage is abject terror. In consequence, however, of this elevated arrangement, there is, from the windows of almost every house, an excellent view; while the succession of visitors constantly passing and re-passing through the place affords, besides, such a lively scene as is not presented by any other little country town in England.

James Payn: *A Hand-Book to the English Lakes*, 1859.

219

Grandeur and Magnificence

For a writer in 1851, Ambleside was the Shangri-la of the Lakes.

There is no station in the Lake District more desirable for visitors to sojourn at than this, situated as it is in the very centre of hills, woods and lakes. They will never be at a loss for a day's excursion, for whatever road they take, east, west, north or south, there is a delighful variety of walks rustic and romantic, views the most enchanting and picturesque, and, in short, scenery which for its grandeur and magnificence cannot fail to excite feelings of the highest admiration and pleasure. From this place, they may on the same day ascend the lofty summit of the mountain and retire into the shady grove; may follow the windings of some lovely stream and float upon the bosom of the deep blue lake, reflecting on its surface the delightful scenery around.

James Gibson: Hand book to the Lakes, 1851.

Come Rain, Come Shine

Advice to visitors in Ambleside to make the most of the weather still holds good today.

One advice we give you, and by following it you cannot fail to be happy at Ambleside and everywhere else. Whatever the weather be, love, admire and delight in it and vow that you would not change it for the atmosphere of a dream. If it be close, hot, oppressive, be thankful for the faint air that comes down fitfully from cliff and chasm, or the breeze that ever and anon gushes from stream and lake. If the heavens are filled with sunshine and you feel the vanity of parasols, how cool the sylvan shade for ever moistened by the murmurs of that fairy waterfall! Should it blow great guns, cannot you take shelter in yonder magnificent fort, whose hanging battlements are warded even from the thunder-bolt by the dense umbrage of unviolated woods? Rain - rain -

rain - an even down-pour of rain that forces upon you visions of Noah and his ark and the top of Mount Ararat - still, we beseech you, be happy. It cannot last long at that rate; the thing is impossible. Even this very afternoon will the rainbow span the blue entrance into Rydal's woody vale as if to hail the westering sun on his approach to the mountains - and a hundred hill-born torrents will be seen flashing out of the upfolding mists. What a delightful dazzle on the light-stricken river! Each meadow shames the lustre of the emerald; and the soul wishes not for language to speak the pomp and prodigality of colours that Heaven now rejoices to lavish on the grove-girdled Fairfield, who has just tossed off the clouds from his rocky crest.

Mary Gordon: *Christopher North: a Memoir of John Wilson, late Professor of Moral Philosophy in the University of Edinburgh*, 1862.

Dinner and Determination

Helm Crag near Grasmere is a popular climb today - but not in the 1790s. From the valley, its distinctive summit rocks - the Lion and the Lamb, the Howitzer and the Lady at the Organ - are clearly seen.

We went in the morning to Grasmere church. There was a very decent congregation and the singing was old-fashioned and good, and, if it had not been for a certain twang at the beginning of every stave, I should have thought them amongst the best country singers I have heard. The men sat on one side of the aisle, the women on the other, upon rough oak benches, and I could not help observing the smiles interchanged when a couple were asked in marriage.

After as good and well-dressed a dinner at Robert Newton's as a man could wish, we set out to surmount the steep ascent of Helm Crag; but the dinner was so cheap I must mention what it consisted of: roast pike, stuffed; a boiled fowl; veal cutlets and ham; beans and bacon; cabbage; pease and potatoes; anchovy sauce; parsley and butter; plain butter; butter and cheese; wheat bread and oat cake; three cups of preserved gooseberries, with a bowl of rich cream in the centre - for two people at ten pence a head.

We went up a narrow lane that gave us, half a mile from the church, a new view of Grasmere valley, with a perpetual waterfall, justly from its force called White-Churn Gill. It rushes from a crescent-heathed hill and forms one of the most considerable brooks that supplies Grasmere.

The sun was hot and, after a gentle ascent of about a mile, we rested some minutes under a thick hawthorn which we will call the foot of the crag. The projecting point of the first rise looked formidable and not less so, to speak in plain English, from having a complete belly full. However, when people are determined to overcome difficulties, time and circunstances are no obstructions.

We were covered from the wind, and it was so steep we were frequently obliged to stop when we met a narrow shelf, and when we got to the first range of the hill I was glad to throw myself down, panting for relief. The grass was slippery, which we guarded against by forcing our sticks as deep into the ground as we possibly could; and when we had gained the second height, I never remember meeting a more cheerful relief than finding we had got over that part of the hill which kept the wind from us - this not only enlivened us but we opened upon prospects which promised to repay our labour when we had surmounted it.

The pinnacle hanging over our right obliged us to take a sweep but, as we had the wind and a near sight of the top, we found less trouble in this stage than in the others. We were exactly one hour from the hawthorn, which was not from its being a high hill but the steepest in this part of the country, being seldom frequented but by foxes, sheep and ravens. Our guide was never on it but once and neither he nor Partridge [another guide] remember that it has been visited by strangers.

Joseph Budworth: *A Fortnight's Ramble to the Lakes*, 1795.

Lofty Thoughts

Climbing Scafell Pike, England's highest mountain, can be therapeutic.

The view afforded from the summit of this lofty mountain is universally allowed to be unequalled in England for extent and variety; much of its grandeur is to be attributed to its superiority in height over every other elevation south of the Scottish Highlands. Although situated in the vicinity of many of the most lofty hills in the Lake District, it so far o'ertops them all as to command an almost unlimited range of country; and we gaze around upon countless peaks, diminished in importance because overlooked, but nevertheless of sufficient grandeur in their own neighbourhood to entitle them to respect here. Between this ocean of hills, the eye travels in complete amaze: here, separated from each other by feaful precipices of a depth sickening to look at; there, slanting like huge waves, to rise with a more precipitous crest directly in front, bewildering the mind with their number, variety and extent; and it would much puzzle even a good topographer to ascertain and describe the relative position, name and proportion of each, as seen from this wild and majestical throne.

And can there be any gratification so complete as that of having conquered the trifling impediments that one necessarily meets with in a climb to a throne like this? The labour is just sufficiently stimulating to excite both mind and body, and while the limbs move on, as if impelled by no agency of the brain, the mind is left free to roam in wildest liberty, drinking new pleasure from every fresh object and rioting in the full enjoyment of the senses apart from every aching care and gnawing influence that affect man's existence.

Commend me, above all things, to a mountain for a cure against ill-humour or ill anything, and if the patient be not half-freed from the malady by the time he has half-climbed the hill-side, he is not *worthy* a doctor, and should needs cure himself by no other agency than his wits, for an the doctor get but hold, he will scarcely part company until his place is changed by the somewhat more useful undertaker.

J. Onwhyn Onwhyn's Pocket Guide to the Lakes, 1841

Severe Fatigue

Not everyone would echo the praises of Scafell Pike.

I do not think, however, that the tourist is repaid for the severe fatigue encountered in the ascent of this mountain; certainly it is the highest summit in England and the view is wonderfully extensive, but everything being so far below the eye, the prospect is not all agreeable, nor is the beauty of the scene at all increased by the bare and craggy summits which on every side immediately surround him.

George Tattersall: *The Lakes of England*, 1836

A Cheap Holiday

An eight-day tour in the 1870s was not expensive.	£	s.	d.
Return ticket Manchester to Lake Side	0	8	6
Second class steamer Lake Side to Bowness	0	1	0
Second class steamer Bowness to Ambleside	0	0	9
Hotel bill at Bowness or Ambleside	0	9	0
Half share of boat on Ullswater	0	1	6
Half share of tip to attendant for seeing Aira Force	0	0	6
Hotel bill, Ullswater	0	8	3
Half share of guide over Helvellyn	0	5	0
Half share of tip at Rydal Fall	0	0	6
Hotel bill, Grasmere	0	10	0
Coach fare Grasmere to Keswick	0	3	6
Half share of boat on lake	0	0	6
Half share of guide up Skiddaw	0	2	6
Hotel bill, Keswick	0	10	6
Buttermere drive	0	5	0
Half tip at Barrow Waterfall	0	0	6
Dinner at Buttermere	0	3	0
Tip to driver of Buttermere coach	0	1	0
Hotel bill, Borrowdale or Rosthwaite	0	7	6
Half share of guide over Stake Pass	0	3	9
Dinner at Dungeon Ghyll Hotel	0	3	0

Hotel bill, etc, Coniston	0 11 0
Third class, Coniston to Furness Abbey	0 1 7
Hotel bill, Furness Abbey	0 8 0
Third class, Furness Abbey to Lake Side	0 1 3½
	5 8 1½
Sundries	7 4½
Total	5 15 6

John Bradbury: *The English Lakes: how to see them for 5½ guineas*, 1872

Seeing the Sights

Among the many curiosities on display for the tourist, one of the most popular was (and still is) the Bowder Stone in Borrowdale. Southey's fictitious Spanish visitor, Don Manuel Alvarez Espriella, was duly scathing, amused and amazed.

Another mile of broken ground, the most interesting which I ever traversed, brought us to a single rock called the Bowder Stone, a fragment of great size which has fallen from the heights. The same person [i.e. Mr Pocklington] who formerly disfigured the island in Keswick Lake with so many abominations has been at work here also; has built a little mock hermitage, set up a new druidical stone, erected an ugly house for an old woman to live in, who is to show the rock, for fear travellers should pass under it without seeing it, cleared away all the fragments round it and, as it rests upon a narrow base like a ship upon its keel, dug a hole underneath through which the curious may gratify themselves by shaking hands with the old woman.

The oddity of this amused us greatly, provoking as it was to meet with such hideous buildings in such a place - for the place is as beautiful as eyes can behold or imagination conceive. The river flows immediately below, of that pale gray green transparency which we

225

sometimes see in the last light of the evening sky; a shelf of pebbles on the opposite shore shows where it finds its way through a double channel when swollen by rains. The rest of the shore is covered with a grove of young trees which reach the foot of a huge single crag, half-clothed with brush-wood - this crag [i.e.Castle Crag] when seen from Keswick appears to block up the pass. Southward, we looked down into Borrowdale, whither we were bound - a vale which appeared in the shape of a horse-shoe.

Robert Southey: *Letters from England, by Don Manuel*
Alvarez Espriella, 1807

A National Asset

The National Trust is one of the prime conservation organisations in the Lake District. One of its founders was Canon Rawnsley: here he celebrates the opening of Brandelhow by Derwentwater, the first trust property in Lakeland.

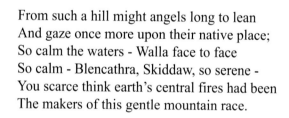

From such a hill might angels long to lean
And gaze once more upon their native place;
So calm the waters - Walla face to face
So calm - Blencathra, Skiddaw, so serene -
You scarce think earth's central fires had been
The makers of this gentle mountain race.

And here may mortals, weary of the strife
Of inconsiderate cities, hope to come
And lean the fair tranquillities of earth;
Here men may pray, here poet-thoughts have birth,
Here all shy forest-creatures find a home,
And wild-wood pleasures help the Nation's life.

Opening of Brandelhow, 16th October 1902 in E.R.
Rawnsley *Canon Rawnsley*, 1923.

226

Table of Authors and Sources

227